Opening Doors,
Opening Opportunities

Related Titles of Interest

Opening Doors, Opening Opportunities

Family Literacy in an Urban Community

Jeanne R. Paratore

Boston University

Allyn and Bacon

Boston ▪ London ▪ Toronto ▪ Sydney ▪ Tokyo ▪ Singapore

Series editor: Arnis E. Burvikovs
Series editorial assistant: Patrice Mailloux
Marketing manager: Kathleen Morgan

Copyright © 2001 by Allyn & Bacon
A Pearson Education Company
Needham Heights, MA 02494

Internet: www.abacon.com

Library of Congress Cataloging-in-Publication Data

Paratore, Jeanne R.
    Opening doors, opening opportunities : family literacy in an urban community / Jeanne R. Paratore.
        p. cm.
    Includes bibliographical references.
    ISBN 0-205-27492-7
    1. Family literacy programs—Massachusetts—Boston—Case studies.   2. Urban education—Massachusetts—Boston—Case studies.   3. Minorities—Education—Massachusetts—Boston—Case studies.   I. Title.

LC153.B7 P37 2001
379.2'4'0974461—dc21   00-064289

Printed in the United States of America

10   9   8   7   6   5   4   3   2   04   03   02   01

To my parents, Marion and Dominick Riccardi

CONTENTS

Preface   ix

Acknowledgments   xi

List of Figures and Tables   xiii

1 Understanding Culturally and Linguistically Diverse Families and Family Literacies   1

Literacy in the Twenty-first Century   1
What Does It Mean to Be Literate?   4
Learning about Families and Family Literacies   7
Family Literacy Programs as a Bridge between Home and School   16

2 The Intergenerational Literacy Project   19

The Community   19
Guiding Educational Principles   21
The Principles in Action   30
Summary   52

3 Is It Working? Reviewing the Evidence   53

Theoretical Assumptions   54
Assessment Measures We Use   56
What Have We Learned?   56
Summary of the Evidence   81

4 Bringing Parents and Teachers Together to Help Children Learn   83

Parents' Perceptions of Roles and Responsibilities   84
The Importance of the Actions Teachers Take   85
Acting on the Evidence: Home–School Partnerships
   and the Intergenerational Literacy Project   88
Summary   98

5 **Learning and Thinking about Families, Schools, and Communities   100**

　　Learning about Adult and Family Literacies   100
　　Learning about Family Literacy Programs   104
　　Learning about Children and School Literacies   108
　　Learning about Home–School Partnerships   109
　　Looking Back and Looking Forward   111

APPENDIX A   Learner Intake Interview   113

APPENDIX B   Learner Exit Interview   121

APPENDIX C   Writing Evaluation Rubric   127

APPENDIX D   Teacher Seminar Readings   129

References   131

Index   139

PREFACE

When I came here I thought that it was going to be easy but it was very difficult. First I didn't speak English. I didn't have friends, and my parents were not here with me. Here life is very different. I have to speak English. I have to go to school. I need to learn to write and read in English. I need to speak with people. Sometimes when I need help I don't know how to say things. I don't understand how to write in a journal. Now I am in school and I want to learn a lot to work in my profession and to have friends and better opportunity, someday to be with my family and to work hard to get a lot of money.

— Parent, Intergenerational Literacy Project, 1998, p. 118

My work . . . had a profound impact on my goals and my view of the world. . . . I learned a great deal about risk taking from the learners in my class who showed a fierce determination to make life better for their children.

— Teacher, Intergenerational Literacy Project

[I am] realizing for the first time in my life, the power we can have to promote change.

— Tutor, Intergenerational Literacy Project

. . . It [Family Literacy Portfolio Project] gave me a whole new view of what she [the parent] does at home. I mean I would've never thought . . . I was glad to know that she was doing that at home but I would've never thought that she would have done that extensively on her own.

— Teacher, Chelsea Public Schools

The first quotation was taken from an essay written by a parent during a family literacy class at the Boston University–Chelsea Public Schools Intergenerational Literacy Project (ILP). The second was written by a Boston University graduate student who taught at the ILP for two years. The third was written by a Boston University undergraduate student who had spent three of his four undergraduate years as a tutor in the ILP—absent only during the year he studied abroad. The fourth was shared by an elementary teacher who had participated in a family literacy portfolio project with an ILP parent.

When the project was conceived in 1989, the reciprocity in learning evident in the collected comments was not among our stated goals. Instead, we set out to provide a service to parents—mothers and fathers who were new immigrants to the United States and so were unfamiliar with the English language and English literacy and with the American schools their children attended. We anticipated helping them become better readers and writers and, through them, helping their children achieve success in school. We did not expect that the project would change those of us who taught—

change our understanding of the families who participated; of literacy and how it is used in different families, in different communities, in different lives; and of ourselves as teachers and learners. It did all of that. In the pages that follow, I tell how the project developed and how we came to understand that in this project, all participants—parents, children, teachers, and tutors—were learners.

Chapter 1 addresses the current debate in family literacy education in the United States: the dissonance in goals and purposes across different programs and in perceptions of the families the programs intend to serve. A review of the existing professional literature provides a foundation for understanding the meaning of literacy in the twenty-first century and the place of literacy in the lives of the linguistically and culturally different families most often served by family literacy programs.

Chapter 2 describes the Intergenerational Literacy Project—the community in which it is situated, the educational principles that provide its foundation, and the instructional and assessment strategies and practices that frame daily classes. I use learners' work to illustrate typical routines and instructional activities. Choosing representative samples was difficult—the few examples chosen were selected from countless possibilities.

Chapter 3 focuses on evaluation of the project, beginning with the theoretical assumptions that undergird the assessment plan. Data are used to describe the characteristics of the learners served by the project during its first ten years, to examine program effectiveness, and to examine group outcomes. Case studies of three learners provide a window into the meaning of the project in individual lives.

Chapter 4 looks beyond the focus on family literacy to the related issue of establishing partnerships between parents and their children's teachers. Following a review of research related to parents' perceptions of their roles in their children's learning and the importance of teachers' actions in parental involvement, two special ILP projects are described: the Parents as Classroom Storybook Project and the Family Literacy Portfolio Project. Each offered parents and teachers particular ways to work together to advance each other's understanding of family and school literacies.

Finally, in Chapter 5, I consider what we learned in the ILP and how it connects to what others have taught us about adult and family literacies, family literacy programs, children and school literacies, and home–school partnerships.

In bringing all of this work together in a single text, I have attempted to honor the work of the more than 1,300 families who have participated in the ILP; the many undergraduate and graduate students at Boston University who have served as co-researchers, teachers, and tutors; and the classroom teachers in the Chelsea Public Schools who worked with us to open doors for linguistically and culturally different parents and their children. There is much work yet to be done if we are to understand fully how to bridge the gap between home and school for nonmainstream families. I offer the ideas in this book as one step toward that goal.

ACKNOWLEDGMENTS

Although I have written this text on my own, within its pages I often use the pronoun *we*. As hard as I tried to revert to the use of the singular pronoun, I was not able to do so, and the reason is simple. None of this work was accomplished alone. From the first day, the Intergenerational Literacy Project was a collaborative effort. Along the way, the collaborators' names and faces changed, as Boston University graduate and undergraduate students have come and gone, as Chelsea Public School teachers and administrators have come and gone, and as parents and children have come and gone. But through it all, each innovation, each finding, each interpretation, each conclusion has been accomplished in concert with others. There are far too many to name individually, and so I will express my gratitude to all of the teachers and tutors who dedicated their time, expertise, and thoughtful reflection to making the Intergenerational Literacy Project work; to administrators and classroom teachers in the Chelsea Public Schools who opened their hearts and minds to the project; to the many foundations and agencies that provided generous funding for both service and research activities; and, most particularly, to Dr. Barbara Krol-Sinclair, who joined the project in 1991 as a literacy teacher and now serves as its project director. Her dedication to the parents, teachers, and tutors is surpassed by none.

LIST OF FIGURES
AND TABLES

Figure 2.1	Guiding Educational Principles	34
Figure 2.2	Sample Completed Literacy Log	36
Figure 2.3	Flexible Grouping and Instructional Framework for Reading Lessons	38
Figure 2.4	Unedited Journal Entry	41
Figure 2.5	Sample Completed Self-assessment	45
Figure 2.6	Sample Completed Shared Storybook Reading Response	47
Figure 2.7	Parent's Letter to a Teacher	48
Figure 2.8	Teacher's Response to Parent's Letter	49
Figure 2.9	Suggestions for Family Literacy Activities Related to Book of the Week	50
Figure 2.10	Printed Label to Affix to Child's Cumulative School Record	51
Figure 3.1	Assessment Measures	58
Figure 3.2	Weekly Family Literacy Practices	63
Figure 3.3	Types of Daily Parent–Child Literacy Interactions	64
Figure 3.4	Types of Weekly Parent–Child Literacy Interactions	65
Figure 3.5	Teachers' Report of Children's School Achievement	66
Figure 3.6	Teachers' Report of Children's End-of-year Reading Achievement	66
Figure 3.7	Parents' Report of Children's School Achievement	67
Figure 3.8	Hung Mei's Dialogue Journal Entry	73
Figure 3.9	Ruth's Dialogue Journal Response to Hung Mei	74
Figure 3.10	The Lesson That Followed the Dialogue	75
Figure 3.11	Hung Mei's Letter to Her Daughter's Teacher	76
Figure 3.12	Hung Mei's Storybook Reading Response	77
Figure 3.13	Silvia's Literacy Log	79
Figure 4.1	Parents' Perceptions of the Purposes of a Family Literacy Portfolio	93
Table 3.1	Family Roles	57
Table 3.2	Countries of Origin of Families in the Intergenerational Literacy Project	60
Table 3.3	First Languages Spoken by Families in the Intergenerational Literacy Project	61

Opening Doors,
Opening Opportunities

1 Understanding Culturally and Linguistically Diverse Families and Family Literacies

Literacy in the Twenty-first Century

As we enter the twenty-first century, the face of American education is changing. The most recent report from the National Center for Education Statistics (1999b) indicates that 36 percent of students enrolled in public elementary and secondary schools were considered part of a minority group in 1996, a reported increase of 12 percent from 1976. The change was largely due to growth in the percentage of Hispanic students, increasing in inner-city public schools from approximately one out of every ten in 1972 to approximately one out of every four in 1996. In the 500 largest school districts, minority students are actually the majority, representing more than 56 percent of the total school population.

At the same time that the number of minority students is increasing, results from the most recent National Assessment of Educational Progress (NAEP) (Donohue, Voelkl, Campbell, & Mazzeo, 1999) indicate that little progress has been made in diminishing the achievement gap between White and minority students. At grades 4, 8, and 12, Black and Hispanic students continue to achieve at the lowest levels in reading in substantially larger numbers than their White peers. The consequences of the low rates of performance are evident in school dropout rates, which reveal minority students to be disproportionately represented: in four states with high proportions of minority enrollments, 70 percent or more of the dropouts were minority students (National Center for Education Statistics, 1999a). Secada, Chavez-Chavez, Garcia, Muñoz, Oakes, Santiago-Santiago, and Slavin (1998) reported that the dropout rate is especially high among Hispanic students, reaching "a staggering 30 percent" (p. 5) when all immigrants (those who attended and left and those who never enrolled) are counted.

Attempts to explain low achievement have often turned to the role parents play in children's learning. Accordingly, the NAEP examined the relationship between home support for literacy and children's performance. At grades 4, 8, and 12, results indicated that students who reported having discussions with their parents about their schoolwork almost every day or once or twice a week had higher average scores than their peers who reported discussing their studies only once or twice a month or less frequently. In addition, as has been the case in earlier assessments, results indicated that at grades 8 and 12, students who reported higher levels of parental education had higher average reading scores.

The assessment also investigated the relationship between family income and reading achievement and found that among fourth graders who were eligible for the free/reduced-price lunch component of the National School Lunch Program, a program that subsidizes lunches to children residing in families near or below the poverty level, 58 percent performed below the Basic level and 2 percent were at the Advanced level, compared with 27 percent and 10 percent, respectively, for those not eligible for free/reduced-price lunch.

The low rates of achievement of so many poor and minority children and the correlation between the children's school performance and parental education and income have led many educators to seek educational alternatives that address the family unit rather than the child alone. St. Pierre, Layzer, and Barnes (1998) identified such programs as "two-generation programs" that are intended to "solve the problems of parents and children in two contiguous generations—to help young children get the best possible start in life and, at the same time, to help their parents become economically self-sufficient" (p. 101). Gadsden (1994) explained the assumption of reciprocity inherent in intergenerational learning programs:

> The traditional unidirectionality of influence going from the parent to the child is broadened, and learning and developmental processes of children, for example, are seen as potentially having an impact on the parents' adult development. Individuals and their contexts are thought to have a reciprocal, continuous, and mutual influence. (p. 12)

Among the earliest proponents of intergenerational education programs was Thomas Sticht, who, with Barbara McDonald in 1992, explained the rationale:

> It is well established that many children arrive at kindergarten or first grade with knowledge, language, and cognitive skills that are different from those needed to acquire higher levels of literacy, mathematics, and critical thinking abilities within the cultural context of mainstream public education. These children frequently fall behind in school and later drop out. They become the marginally literate and marginally employable youth and adults who comprise some one-fifth to one-third of the adult population in the U.S. . . . Many of these young adults become parents of children and are unable to transmit educationally relevant preschool oral and written language skills, which are the foundation for later reading and writing skills, or to model reasoning and thinking skills, frequently using mathematical concepts. Without these basics in language, numeracy and critical thinking, the children from these homes show up for school prepared to recapitulate the failure of their parents, and the cycle repeats itself. (p. 1)

Since 1979, when Sticht first called for an intergenerational approach to the educational issues that confront so many adults and children (Sticht, Beeler, & McDonald, 1992), family literacy programs have proliferated in schools and communities across the United States and, at the same time, have become the focus of vigorous debate. Many see them as a panacea—the answer to a host of problems associated with school failure (Hendrix, 1999). In her presidential address to the National Center for Family Literacy Annual Conference in 1997, just months after the U.S. Congress had passed a welfare reform bill, Sharon Darling described family literacy as "the most powerful welfare reform strategy" (p. 3) and family literacy programs as "uniquely positioned to move families to self-sufficiency while building a strong family system" (p. 2). She noted:

> Study after study has shown the inextricable link between chronic welfare dependency and intergenerational undereducation. The most basic measures indicate that many welfare recipients need to improve their literacy skills in order to succeed in the workplace. For example, almost 90% of the people who have the lowest level of literacy skills, and almost 70% of those in the second lowest level, are either unemployed or have an income that ranks in the lowest 20% of the population. And our own studies from NCFL . . . show that family literacy can make a difference. We have long-term evidence that family literacy not only helps families with educational obstacles, but also moves them from welfare dependency to self-sufficiency, while at the same time strengthening the family. Our long-term research has shown that family literacy reduces dependency on public assistance by 50% and increases unemployment significantly. (p. 3)

Others, however, strongly disagree with the claim that education will provide a shield against poverty. As reported by the National Center for Children in Poverty (1999), data from a study of patterns and trends of poverty in the United States indicate a sharp increase in poverty rates for young children whose parents went to college but did not graduate and for young children whose parents completed high school but did not attend college. The evidence led to the conclusion that "it is clear that a high school diploma or even some college education has become far less likely to protect a family against poverty" (p. 3).

In a book published at just about the same time that Darling delivered her address, Denny Taylor (1997) argued:

> The premise that a lack of facility with literacy is causally related not only to poverty, but also to underemployment, low educational achievement, crime, the breakdown of the family, and the decline of moral standards is the result of faulty reasoning that enables us to abdicate responsibility and blame the family for these societal problems. The recent focus on family literacy that is seemingly designed to bring more literacy to parents and children is an effort to shift the blame for poverty and underemployment onto the people least responsible for and least able to struggle against the systematic inequalities of modern societies. (p. 2)

Auerbach (1997) also challenged the belief that literacy training will lead to self-sufficiency:

> Census statistics . . . indicate that race and gender override education as determinants of income and job status (white males with high school diplomas have higher mean incomes than African American males with college degrees or women of any race with graduate degrees). Ethnographic research on the relationship between literacy training and job retention suggests that literacy skills per se may not be the critical factor. (p. 77)

Valdés (1996) cautioned that those who advocate parent involvement as a way to break the cycle of low academic achievement and, ultimately, the cycle of poverty are well intentioned but misguided:

> They are subscribing to existing mythologies about the power of school to right all social wrongs, and they are failing to take into account how social inequalities, educational ideologies, educational structures, and interpersonal interactions work together to affect educational outcomes. (p. 195)

What accounts for such divergent and discrepant views of family literacy and of the goals of family literacy programs? Perhaps, at the core of the disagreement, are differences in our most basic understandings. What, for example, is meant by the term *literacy?* What do we know of the families who are most often identified as in need of family literacy interventions? How do our understandings of the meanings of literacy and of the literate lives of the families we intend to serve influence the ways we choose to teach them? In the remainder of this chapter, these are the questions that I will try to answer.

What Does It Mean to Be Literate?

At the heart of understanding and reconciling the apparent differences in representations of family literacy is the need to acquire a shared definition of the term *literacy.* Although policymakers increasingly rely on standardized assessment to both define and measure the literacy proficiency of children and adults, most literacy experts view such measures as wholly inadequate and agree that accurate definition is a far more complex and appropriate measurement and far more varied than such tests provide. Wagner (1991) noted the difficulty inherent in defining *literacy:*

> "Literacy" is a remarkable term. While seeming to refer to simple individual possession of the complementary mental technologies of reading and writing, literacy is not only difficult to define in individuals and delimit within societies, but it is also charged with emotional and political meaning. It was not long ago that newspapers and scholars referred to whole societies as "illiterate and uncivilized" as a single referent and "illiterate" is still a term which carries a negative connotation. . . . (p. 12)

A review of the definitions of *literacy* that have emerged in the last two decades documents the complexity noted by Wagner. In an essay prepared for the Center for the Book at the Library of Congress, Asheim (1987) defined literacy not as a uniform quality but rather as one that is "tied to a way of thinking, an acceptance of conventions of the form, and a mind set" (p. 15). Gee (1989) argued that literacy is more than just reading and writing, that it is a part of a larger discourse, a "way of being . . . a socially accepted association among ways of using language, of thinking and of acting that can be used to identify oneself as a member of a socially meaningful group or 'social network'" (p. 180). Like Gee, Ferdman (1990) examined literacy in the context of culture, and he concluded that being viewed as literate in a particular society requires far more than mastery over representational symbols:

> In addition to being skilled in the use of methods of representation such as the alphabet, writing implements, books, and so on, the literate person must be familiar with a particular configuration of meanings in context, to comprehend appropriately the content of what is encoded and decoded. Becoming literate means developing mastery not only over processes, but also over the symbolic media of the culture—the ways in which cultural values, beliefs, and norms are represented. Being literate implies actively maintaining contact with collective symbols and the processes by which they are represented. Thus, literacy goes beyond superficial transactions with a printed or written page and extends into the ability to comprehend and manipulate its symbols—the words and concepts—and to do so in a culturally prescribed manner. (p. 188)

Ferdman further emphasized the active nature of literacy and explained that being literate was not a quality one possesses but rather represents actions one takes: "being literate means engaging in particular activities that so define persons as they transact with the social environment" (p. 181).

Several researchers have defined literacy as multifaceted. Akinnaso (1991) noted that

> literacy defies a monolithic definition. Rather, it is conceived of as a range of socially constructed practices, values, and competencies regarding reading and writing as activities as well as certain ways of speaking. The quality and quantity of these activities are hopelessly variable, as are their effective participants. (p. 74)

In more recent work, Courtney Cazden and a group of ten colleagues (New London Group, 1996) challenged educators to rethink their conceptualization of literacy and, subsequently, literacy pedagogy "to include negotiating a multiplicity of discourses" (p. 61). They argued that such a stance is important to account for both the increased cultural and linguistic diversity of our society and the "burgeoning variety of text forms associated with information and multimedia technologies" (p. 61). They explained that the singular term *literacy* remains centered on language only, while *multiliteracies* represent "modes of representation much broader than language alone. These differ according to culture and context, and have specific cognitive, cultural, and social effects" (p. 64). Further, they argued:

Effective citizenship and productive work now require that we interact effectively using multiple languages, multiple Englishes, and communication patterns that more frequently cross cultural, community, and national boundaries. Subcultural diversity also extends to the ever broadening range of specialist registers and situational variations in language, be they technical, sporting, or related to groups of interest and affiliation. When the proximity of cultural and linguistic diversity is one of the key facts of our time, the very nature of language learning has changed. (p. 64)

With this view of literacy as a backdrop—a view marked by the understanding that literacy is multifaceted and that its acquisition and use are shaped by social, cultural, and political conditions—the tension that surrounds family literacy interventions may begin to come into focus and to be understood. For those who view literacy in this context, changing one's literacy means more than changing one's scores on standardized tests and measures. Rather, as Wagner (1991) noted:

Any attempt to intervene in order to change an individual's literacy status means change not only in a set of etic skills (as measured by most tests and taught in most schools), but also in the emic, socially constructed and mediated behaviors and beliefs that define each individual, the rest of his or her community, and ultimately, the communities and societies themselves. (p. 19)

Fundamentally, making changes in one's literacy actions and interactions, Wagner argued, "is to change the individual and ourselves" (p. 19). Accepting this view of literacy, in turn, influences how educators perceive their own roles and responsibilities in the lives of the children and adults they teach. Gee (1999) argued that if one accepts this definition of literacy,

One cannot coherently debate ways of improving reading and leave out social, cultural, institutional, and political issues and interventions as if they were "separate" from literacy (mere "background noise" as it were). (p. 360)

Gee's comments serve as a reminder of a caution issued by Purves (1991) years earlier about the power of literacy education:

The activity of being literate . . . is a deliberate and social activity, one that takes place in the world; it should not be seen as an abstracted mental state or condition. Those who are involved in literacy education should, therefore, be aware of their social responsibility. (p. 51)

It is the acknowledgment of social responsibility, of the potential for literacy intervention programs and the particular uses of literacy that they advocate to intrude on the very fabric of family lives, that has caused some researchers to argue that family literacy researchers and practitioners must tread cautiously. Citing Bronfenbrenner (1979), Valdés (1996) contended that we "still lack the kinds of knowledge" (p. 40) to which he referred when he wrote:

I shall presume to speak for the profession in pointing out what we do know and what we don't. We know a great deal about children's behavior and development, and quite a bit about what can and does happen inside of families—parent child interaction, family dynamics, and all that. But we know precious little about the circumstances under which families live, how these circumstances affect their lives, and what might happen if the circumstances were altered. . . . Before we can engage in parent education of the kinds here proposed, we have to learn a good deal more than we know at present about the actual experience of families in different segments of our society. (p. 220)

During the years since Bronfenbrenner wrote these words, several researchers have attempted to learn more about the nonmainstream families that are most often the focus of family literacy intervention programs. In many cases, researchers have relied on ethnography as research methodology and sociocultural theory as a viewing lens to gain understanding about people different from them. Purcell-Gates (1996) explained:

To understand and gain useful insights into literacy learning, one must explore the classroom settings and other settings within which people learn to read and write. This exploration includes describing how literacy is defined in each setting, what counts as literacy knowledge, who gets to participate in events, and how this participation is defined. The goal is to understand how the participants perceive, interpret, and evaluate what they are doing.

It is this sociocultural theoretical lens, I believe, that gives us the best chance of understanding the low literacy attainment by poor and minority peoples. How can we understand why so many children do not learn what the mainstream schools think they are teaching unless we can get "inside" the learners and see the world through their eyes? If we do not try to do this, if we continue to use the mainstream experience of reality as the perspective, we fool ourselves into believing that we are looking through a window when instead we are looking into a mirror. Our explorations threaten to reflect only ourselves and our world, serving no real explanatory purpose. (p. 6)

In the section that follows, I report on several ethnographies in which researchers have studied minority families and the ways in which literacy shapes their lives.

Learning about Families and Family Literacies

In her seminal work on family literacy, Taylor (1983) defined her goal as the systematic examination of "reading and writing activities that have consequences in and are affected by family life" (Preface). She noted that she hoped others would join her in this work so that all could learn more about the "many ways children growing up in a variety of settings initiate, absorb, and synthesize the cultural complexities of learning to read and write" (Preface). Within these early words about family literacy was the clear, though perhaps implicit, message that different families acquire and use literacy in different ways. In her initial investigation of families chosen because they had a child who was successfully learning to read and write, Taylor observed the ways in which literacy events were seamlessly woven within the daily activities and routines of family members. She noted the many advantages the children enjoyed as they entered school settings for which they had been well prepared, and she pondered the consequences for children whose family lives were far more disparate with the educational system. She wondered if the current adult literacy and parent educational programs were "too literally literate" (p. 88) and commented:

> It is entirely possible that the undue emphasis on specific didactic encounters might unwittingly undermine the opportunity for reading and writing to become socially significant in the lives of both adults and children, and therefore an integral facet of family life. (p. 88)

Since Taylor's early musings, what have we learned about the literacies of linguistically and culturally different families and families who are undereducated and living in poverty? What have researchers taught us about the ways diverse families use literacy in the course of their daily lives, and what have they taught us about the ways linguistically and culturally different parents view schools and their children's learning?

Heath's (1983) landmark study of two working-class communities, one Black, the other White, was among the earliest works to document the language and literacy practices of different cultural groups. Over a ten-year period, Heath studied the children and families of Roadville and Trackton, living just a few miles apart. What was striking about this early work was the evidence that in these communities, where so many children eventually experienced school failure, children's early language learning experiences were rich and varied but also decidedly different. Her findings lead her to conclude:

> Roadville and Trackton residents have a variety of literate traditions, and in each community these are interwoven in different ways with oral uses of language, ways of negotiating meaning, deciding on action, and achieving status. Patterns of using reading and writing in each community are interdependent with ways of using space. . . . Habits of using the written word also develop as they help individuals fulfill self-perceived roles of care giving and preparing children for school. Roadville parents believe it their task to praise and practice reading with their young children; Trackton adults believe the young have to learn to be and do, and if reading is necessary for this learning, that will come. (p. 234)

In school, the differences in the ways the children had learned to use talk, the ways they had learned to use space, and the ways they had learned to use and respond to books created confusion for both teachers and students. Heath noted that "teachers expressed repeatedly that their problems were not understanding or accepting the forms of the children's language, but in comprehending how and why the children used language as they did" (p. 278).

Heath's work set the stage for others to examine the ways children growing up in nonmainstream families learn to use language and literacy in their daily lives. In 1988, in a three-year ethnographic study, Taylor and Dorsey-Gaines studied six African American children living in urban poverty with their parents. They did not find the literacy-impoverished worlds so many expect of poor, urban families. They found, instead, that literacy was an "integral part of the children's everyday lives" (p. 61). The children drew pictures and self-portraits, they wrote cards and letters, they read books, and they completed schoolwork. Their parents, too, used literacy frequently and in multiple ways: to complete forms, to make plans and maintain social relationships, to acquire news-related information, to read for pleasure, to check or confirm information, and to fulfill educational requirements. Importantly, they did all of this in the service of what Taylor and Dorsey-Gaines called "genuine purposes": to share an experience, to convey a message, to gain information, or to entertain. Taylor and Dorsey-Gaines observed family members to be "active members in a print community in which literacy is used for a wide variety of social, technical, and aesthetic purposes, for a wide variety of audiences, and in a wide variety of situations" (p. 200). They concluded:

> Education and literacy cannot be used interchangeably. We found family members who were highly literate, and yet they were not educated in the traditional sense of the word. (p. 202)

In an ethnography of Latino families, Delgado-Gaitan (1990) examined the ways in which Mexican, Spanish-speaking families assisted their children with literacy learning at home and with schooling in general. The 20 families she studied lived in Portillo, a multiethnic town that had been home to Mexican immigrants for many generations. The section of town where most of the Mexican families lived was working class, with approximately 90 percent employed in service jobs or as laborers. The members of this community included English-only speakers, bilingual speakers, and limited-English speakers. In the families studied, the majority of adults had fewer than six years of formal education. They all expressed a strong desire for their children to succeed in school, and their desire to help them led many of them to try to improve their English skills by attending classes in English as a second language. Consistent with the findings of other studies of Latino families (e.g., Valdés, 1996), for these families, *buena educación* (good education) represented far more than effective schooling in the American sense; it also included acquisition of values such as respect, discipline, and cooperation.

The school system the children attended was locally and nationally recognized as an effective and creative program for both English and Spanish speakers. Of particular note was a Spanish-only preschool program that was successful in closing the gap previously registered between English- and Spanish-speaking children on entry into kindergarten. In addition to its emphasis on first language learning, the preschool also placed a strong emphasis on educating parents to be co-teachers of their children. Toward this end, parents were invited to attend monthly meetings to learn about the school curriculum and ways to reinforce it at home in the course of their daily activities.

In this aspect of her work, Delgado-Gaitan focused on 20 children in the second and third grades who were having differential success in learning to read. All of the children had received all of their schooling in Portillo. Eleven were characterized as "novice" readers, achieving at least one year below the expected grade level, and nine were characterized as "advanced" readers, achieving at least one year above the expected grade level. The children were observed as they learned about reading and writing both at home and at school. Observations of children's school literacy experiences, and particularly the differences in the instruction of the high- and low-performing students, were largely similar to those reported in previous studies (e.g., Allington, 1983; Hiebert, 1983). That is, novice students spent substantially more time than advanced students on rote memorization of vocabulary, proceeded at a slower pace, and were directed to focus on the explicit and literal information in text. In the cases of both novice and advanced students, little attention was paid to encouraging or instructing children to relate their background knowledge and experience to the texts they were reading in the classroom. In addition, in both cases, children were assigned unfinished classroom tasks as homework.

Delgado-Gaitan's observations of the children at home, like Taylor and Dorsey-Gaines's, were in striking conflict with the often-held view of literacy-impoverished home environments in undereducated, low-income families. She found that parents attempted to support their children's success in school in several ways. They demanded high standards of behavior and instilled respect for adults; they also purchased educational puzzles, storybooks, and, in some cases, even encyclopedias. When book buying was impossible, they brought their children to the library and helped them find books they liked. They were observed reading to their children, a practice that they learned from their contact with the bilingual preschool teachers when their children first entered the school community. Many told favorite stories to their children, continuing the oral tradition of their culture. As with the families in Taylor and Dorsey-Gaines's study, these families used literacy for genuine purposes: they read letters from family members in Mexico and wrote letters in return. When family members were English-speaking, they often used letter writing as a way to practice their English. Talk was important in these families. They spoke about their feelings and experiences, about the stories they read and heard, and about the ways their own experiences related to the texts.

Homework played an important role in the conduct of home literacy, and in many ways changed it. When possible, the parents helped with homework, and when homework was too difficult for them to do, they shifted their emphasis to reminding or motivating their children to study. Delgado-Gaitan (1990) noted:

> Parents participated differently with their children on homework literacy tasks, although the majority shared a feeling of confusion as a result of unclear school expectations and vagueness about the meaning of homework. Feelings of incompetence in their ability to help their children perpetuated a sense of isolation among the families. They felt responsible for their children's failure. The feeling of shame about being poor and lacking formal educational skills restricted their use of school and community resources. (p. 115)

In observing home–school communication, Delgado-Gaitan found frequent confusion and misunderstanding. Contrary to teacher beliefs, frequency of contact was often a poor measure of the parents' involvement in or commitment to their children's education. Unlike parents who were themselves schooled in the United States, many of these Mexican parents had little or no familiarity with the expectation that parents should maintain frequent contact with their children's teachers. There was an assumption that the teacher knows best, that whatever the teacher says is accurate, and that the teacher's directions should simply be followed. In response to notes that were sent home, parents admonished children to try harder and often monitored their homework more closely, but the parents were often unaware of the expectation that they should follow up or contact the teacher for additional information.

In addition, parents sometimes found mixed messages in the school's actions. On the one hand, the school seemed to encourage parent involvement and participation. On the other hand, parents were frustrated by the seemingly insufficient time to discuss their children's progress during parent–teacher conferences.

Of the many important findings in Delgado-Gaitan's work, three stand out. First, these families were clearly committed to and actively involved in supporting their children's success in school and did so not only by implementing literacy practices taught to them by preschool teachers but also by engaging children in numerous literacy interactions that were part of their family traditions and routines. Second, intensive efforts by the school system during the children's preschool year to introduce parents to ways to support their children's school success were effective in helping parents add to their routine literacy interactions with their children. There was ample evidence that parents had learned to embed the literacy practices taught to them without displacing their own family routines and traditions. Third, despite the carefully planned, thoughtful, and collaborative co-teaching approach during the children's preschool year, there remained areas of misunderstanding and confusion that often went unaddressed in later school years.

Valdés (1996) also examined the lives of Mexican American families to "discover how bilingual language and literacy skills developed in newly arrived immigrant children outside the school setting" (p. xv). Valdés studied ten families who lived in the same community, or *el barrio*, situated just a few hours from the Mexican border in a large urban state. Nine of the ten families were two-parent families. Of the 19 parents, only one was born in the United States, but they differed widely in the number of years they had lived in the United States, with a range of 4 to 38 years. They also differed in English proficiency: many spoke English quite well; some, not at all. And they differed in their educational backgrounds and literacy abilities. Some had some schooling in their own countries; others had none. Some read well in Spanish; others, not at all. The husbands worked as unskilled laborers: farm laborers, construction workers, domestic servants, yard maintenance workers.

Like the mothers in Portillo, these mothers "considered la educación de los hijos [the moral education of their children] to be their primary responsibility" (p. 125). Of importance is Valdés's description of the children's interaction in the family:

> "Respeto" for the mother's role was very much in evidence in what children did *not* do . . . even children under two years old did not interrupt conversations between their mother and other adults. They did not demand attention, act up, or otherwise disturb her. At most, they sat quietly by her side and listened to the conversation. When a

directive was given, it was followed promptly. If a younger child did not do so, an older sibling soon made certain that the youngster did what he had been told. (p. 120)

Valdés paints a portrait of parent–child interaction that is in many ways quite different from the middle-class American family. In these families, children were taught to be highly respectful of adults, generally quiet in their presence, mindful of not making unnecessary demands on their mother's time or attention, attentive to the lessons taught, and aware of their role boundaries. Valdés noted that, unlike children in American families, these Latino children were not asked questions to recount or display their knowledge, but rather so that mothers could gauge their understanding of their roles and responsibilities and provide further guidance. Valdés explained that mothers believed they had prepared their children well for school:

> They had taught them to be respectful, and they had taught them to behave. They did not know that other, more "American" mothers, had also taught their children their colors, letters, and numbers. They naively believed that letters, colors, and numbers were part of what their children would learn in school. (p. 148)

In school, in general, the children in these families did not do well. Valdés suggested that at least part of the reason was children's lack of awareness of the differences between the expectations at home and at school:

> As children trained not to be disruptive, not to call attention to themselves, not to interrupt adult speech, and so forth, they behaved appropriately by following familiar rules of interaction. They did not speak out loud, ask for the teacher's attention, volunteer, or call out answers. They sat quietly, taking everything in, and when they had a question, they approached the person that most resembled a family member—the grandmother-like figure of the volunteer aid [sic]—just as they had been trained to do by their mothers in front of company, and they whispered a question or a remark. (p. 147)

Valdés found parents' understandings of American schooling and interactions with teachers marked by confusion and misunderstanding. Invitations to school often went unanswered, sometimes because parents were embarrassed by their lack of English proficiency and little schooling, sometimes because parents had not learned to trust school administrators and teachers and had been told that "harm could be done by a teacher who took a dislike to particular children" (p. 163), and sometimes because parents understood the request for a meeting to be voluntary, not mandatory. On the few occasions when parents initiated a meeting with teachers, it was to discuss their children's behavior, not their academics. Behavior they perceived to be their responsibility, academics as the role of the teacher. To cross boundaries would be, they believed, offensive and inappropriate.

And finally, Valdés explained that beyond these misunderstandings and confusions, the backgrounds and experiences of these families had not taught them that education offered them a way to meet their goals. Energy in these households was not aimed primarily at supporting children in school, as in many middle-class American households, but rather was directed at maintaining "the welfare of the household as a functioning unit" (p. 180). Children could, therefore, be pulled away from schoolwork for a host of reasons: an ill family member, the need to help out in the family business, or an important family event. Unlike their middle-class peers, these immigrant parents could not be counted on to disrupt family affairs and routines to attend to school business: helping children with homework , attending a school event, or purchasing particular items needed for school the next day.

Valdés's work reminds us that understanding the ways linguistically and culturally different parents interact with their children and their children's teachers is not simple. The actions they take at home and at school are driven by a system of attitudes and beliefs that are, in many ways, culturally different from those of mainstream American families. To support children's education in the manner that they are often asked to do means changing the family system in ways that they are unable and perhaps even unwilling to do. Valdés concluded that, although well-intentioned, family intervention programs too often fail to recognize, appreciate, and respect the integrity and legitimacy of established family dynamics.

In contrast to Valdés, who drew attention to the discontinuities between the cultural practices of the Mexican families she studied and those of mainstream families, Vasquez, Pease-Alvarez, and Shannon (1994) focused on areas of congruence and continuity. They argued that

> positioning minority group socialization practices in direct opposition to those of the middle-class home and the school draws attention away from accurate descriptions of those practices and from a consideration of the possibility that other sets of relationships may exist between cultures that operate in close proximity to one another, including accommodation and biculturation. Rather than recognizing multiple perspectives and identities, proponents of the discontinuity view assume that children are forced to choose the school code over the home code. (p. 10)

To support their view that families of different cultures and languages have much in common, these researchers drew upon their data from a series of small, independent studies conducted in a Mexican American community they named Eastside in the San Francisco Bay Area. Like the earlier communities studied, Eastside is multiethnic. Although Mexican-dominated, there are pockets of European American, South American, Southern European, and Pacific Islander families. Most Mexican Americans are first generation, working class, and Spanish speaking, and most have resided in the United States for fewer than 20 years.

Vasquez, Pease-Alvarez, and Shannon found that, like middle-class European American parents, Eastside parents saw themselves "as responsible and deliberate participants in their children's language learning process" (p. 77). They emphasized conversation, starting from the child's earliest months; as children grew older, they questioned them during conversation, requesting elaboration and clarification; they assisted with cues that helped their children to explain or correct their utterances; they provided experiences intended to develop or enhance their children's language development, taking them to the library, reading to them, and supplying crayons, pencils, and papers. They told stories, reconstructing "family history, contemporary events, gossip, and folklore" (p. 121).

As Vasquez, Pease-Alvarez, and Shannon watched children negotiate their daily activities within and outside the community, they concluded that their Spanish language and Latino culture did not serve to isolate or marginalize them, but rather that their bilingualism and biculturalism provided them an important and valuable resource. These children successfully and effectively pooled the English instruction and practice offered to them at school with the Spanish instruction and practice provided at home to negotiate their multiple worlds both for themselves and for their families. Their bilingualism and biculturalism were a plus, not a minus.

These findings led Vasquez, Pease-Alvarez, and Shannon to argue against the "discontinuity perspective" as limiting and even divisive and to propose a "recognition perspective," which

> allows us to replace the portrayal of an immigrant culture as one isolated from its historical and contemporary surroundings with a new vision of a vital culture, rich in linguistic inheritances full of positive and creative possibilities that maintain and at the same time enhance both the home and school cultures and languages. (p. 12)

Luis Moll and his colleagues also used ethnographic methodology to examine Latino households and the "funds of knowledge" within them, defined as "historically accumulated and culturally developed bodies of knowledge and skills essential for household or individual functioning and well-being" (Moll, Amanti, Neff, & Gonzalez, 1992, p. 133). They explained their frame of reference:

> A critical assumption in our work is that educational institutions have stripped away the view of working-class minority students as emerging from households rich in social and intellectual resources. Rather than focusing on the knowledge these students bring to school and using it as a foundation for learning, the emphasis has been on what these students lack in terms of the forms of language and knowledge sanctioned by the schools. This emphasis on "disadvantages" has provided justification and inaccurate portrayals of the children and their families. (Gonzalez et al., 1995, p. 445)

Looking across a series of studies, these researchers reported some basic findings. First, they found that household funds of knowledge are complex—they described them as "flexible, adaptive, and active" involving "multiple persons from outside the homes" (Moll et al., 1992, p. 133). They also characterized the household networks as reciprocal: "Each exchange with relatives, friends, and neighbors entails not only many practical activities . . . but constantly provides contexts in which learning can occur (p. 134). Finally, they reported that the interactions that occur emerge from children's interests and questions: "In contrast to classrooms, knowledge is obtained by the children, not imposed by the adults" (p. 134). They concluded:

> Our analysis of funds of knowledge represents a positive (and, we argue, realistic) view of households as containing ample cultural and cognitive resources with great, potential utility for classroom instruction. . . . This view of households, we should mention,

contrasts sharply with prevailing and accepted perceptions of working class families as somehow disorganized socially and deficient intellectually; perceptions that are well accepted and rarely challenged in the field of education and elsewhere. (p. 134)

These studies of linguistically and culturally different families and the ways they use literacy during the course of their daily lives call to mind the work of Annette Lareau (1989). At the end of her year-long study of high- and low-income families, Lareau concluded:

> Families may be very similar in how much they stress the importance of education or how frequently and diligently they attempt to teach their children new words, but they may differ in how closely these activities are tied to the school's curriculum, how much they monitor their children's school performance, and how much they complain to educators. (p. 170)

Like the families Lareau investigated, the families studied by Heath, Taylor and Dorsey-Gaines, Delgado-Gaitan, Valdés, Vasquez, Pease-Alverez, and Shannon, and Moll and his colleagues were, in many ways, like mainstream parents. Most notably, they were characterized as wanting their children to succeed in school and as attempting to support their children's school success in numerous ways, including buying school-oriented books and toys, reading to children, helping with homework, and exhorting children to do well in school. As well, however, there were many ways in which these parents differed from mainstream parents: they often did not attend school meetings; they typically did not put aside family responsibilities to help with school projects; and they did not question the teacher about particular practices or events. Although in most cases researchers found the children's language learning experiences to be rich and varied, they also often found them to be different from those of mainstream children. They were typically not asked questions that would cause them to recite or display their knowledge; they were often not explicitly taught letter names and sounds, colors, or numbers, and they did not "practice" school-like tasks for the purpose of becoming literate. Rather, they practiced literacy to get things done in the course of their daily lives. The differences led Purcell-Gates (1995) to conclude that an apt description for such children is not illiterate but rather "differently-literate" (p. 184).

The consequences of being differently literate are serious. Unfamiliar with literacy practices common to schools, many children from minority families are judged not ready to learn as they enter schools. In large part, schools attempt to address children's purported lack of readiness by bringing them into compliance with the school's expectations—through early intervention programs, compensatory education programs, and special education programs, in all of which minority children are overrepresented (see, for example, Harry, 1992; Mehan, Villanueva, Hubbard, & Lintz, 1996). Although many of these programs are believed to offer children important opportunities to level the playing field, they have also been criticized as emphasizing "getting the child 'ready' for school, rather than getting the school 'ready' to serve increasingly diverse children" (Swadener & Lubeck, 1995, p. 18). The effects of early intervention programs have been largely uneven and often not sustained through later years of schooling (Barnett, 1998). To the extent that school programs fail to make the literacy curriculum relevant to the home and community lives of the children they serve, Gee (1999) argued that they are wrongheaded:

> Students do not master any school practice without being motivated to enter into and identify with that practice and without believing that they will be able to function within it and use it fruitfully now or in later life. For students . . . questions of identity, motivation, and ability to function are central for learning and literacy. (p. 362)

This brings us back, again, to the apparent divide in the field of family literacy. On the one hand, we have learners who, on many measures, are found to be failing in school—learners who are disproportionately members of economically poor or minority groups. By and large, educators conclude that a primary reason for school failure is inadequate family support and devise programs to "fix" the family by providing instruction in the literacies families do not have. In one publication from the National Center for Family Literacy, the authors commented on the absence of resources available to children of undereducated parents: "Not only do these children lack the advantages of a home with an educated parent, they are also less likely to be exposed to educational opportunities outside the home" (National Center for Family Literacy, nd, p. 5). The focus on the literacies parents do not have has also led to what many would claim are faulty conclusions about nonmainstream parents' aspirations and ambitions for their children and, consequently, to questionable goals for family literacy interventions. Among the "model goals" listed in a 1988–89 report from NCFL was the following:

> Change the system of meaning within the home so children receive messages conveying the importance of education, the value of schooling, the importance of personal responsibility, and hope of achieving education, employment, and a successful adult life. (Darling & Hayes, 1988–89, p. 9)

However, when we take the time to look inside the families and communities of the children who are failing in large numbers, we find that we are wrong—these are not children who come to school deprived of opportunities to learn about literacy and language. Rather, they often have rich and diverse literacy and language backgrounds. Yet, what they bring to school seems to have little payoff for them. What they are taught in school is, in the context of their real lives, unconnected and unconnecting. What can we do? What *should* we do?

Family Literacy Programs as a Bridge between Home and School

In her essay examining the conceptual issues facing the field of family literacy, Gadsden (1994) explained that at the center of the disagreement and dissension that characterize the work in family literacy are two seriously conflicting premises: one that perceives the family's lack of school-like literacy as "an obstacle to overcome in order for learning to occur" (p. 13) and the other that "sees the literacy practices already used in the home . . . as the basis for instruction" (p. 14). Rather than choosing sides in the debate, however, Gadsden argued that both premises may be useful:

> Many parents want assistance in using school-like models for literacy and it is not only possible, but in fact, essential to use parents' knowledge in developing instruction and integrating their interests into the curriculum. The demarcation between the two premises may not be entirely appropriate, however. While the models based on the first premise hold promise for improving the literate abilities of parents and children, models based on the second provide for understanding the family as a source and user of knowledge. What the first may provide us in measurable terms (e.g., test score gains) over the short term, the second may allow us to sustain in interest and participation with family literacy programs. (p. 14)

Strong support for Gadsden's position is found in the work of other researchers and theorists. Speaking of educators' responsibility to explicitly teach children what she referred to as the "codes of power," Delpit (1995) argued that parents have little interest in having the school reinforce what children already know and instead "want to ensure that the school provides their children with discourse patterns, interactional styles, and spoken and written language codes that will allow them success in the larger society" (p. 29). Delgado-Gaitan (1993) also addressed the school's responsibility to teach parents what they need to know to support their children in school. She suggested a critical proposition as a basis for working with parents:

> The knowledge required to participate in schools is socioculturally bound and transmitted in socially constructed settings. Thus, organized efforts are necessary in order to provide parents with explicit knowledge about schools and how the educational system operates. . . . If this information is not made available to all parents, parent participation is limited to those who have the means to gain access. (p. 140)

Delgado-Gaitan argued that her own work in Latino communities in California (1990, 1994, 1996) provided evidence that family literacy classes can serve to empower parents in several ways: the parents with whom she worked learned more about schools and school literacies and therefore gained confidence in their interactions with teachers and administrators; as parents and children spent more time reading and writing together, they created a context for sharing values and opinions about the importance of family; and, in cases where reading with their children was not a common activity prior to parents' participation in literacy classes, parents and children "accepted changes in their family organization to accommodate the new behavior" (1994, p. 167).

Further evidence of the legitimacy of the claim that the two premises about family literacies that often serve to divide educators can be joined effectively can be drawn from other work. Shanahan, Mulhern, and Rodriguez-Brown (1995) explained that Project FLAME (Family Literacy: Apprendiendo, Mejorando, Educando [Learning,

Improving, Education]) was based on some key assumptions: that a supportive home environment is essential to literacy development, that parents can have a positive effect on their children's learning, and that parents who are confident and successful learners will be effective teachers for their children. Studies of outcomes of Project FLAME (Shanahan et al., 1995; Rodríguez-Brown, Li, & Albom, 1999) indicate that it led to improved English proficiency for parents, improvements in children's knowledge of letter names and print awareness, more frequent visits by parents to school, more literacy materials at home, and more confidence in helping with their children's homework. Other initiatives have yielded similarly positive findings, including enhanced opportunities for literacy and biliteracy development (Auerbach, 1992; Quintero & Huerta-Macías, 1990; Quintero & Velarde, 1990; Thornburg, 1993), increased interaction between parents and their children's teachers (Quintero & Huerta-Macías, 1990; Quintero & Velarde, 1990; Thornburg, 1993), increased self-confidence of parents in helping their children with their schoolwork (Ada, 1988; Quintero & Huerta-Macías, 1990; Quintero & Velarde, 1990), and increased understanding of how they are able to support their children's literacy learning (Ada, 1988; Thornburg, 1993).

Like these programs, the Intergenerational Literacy Project, which I began in 1989 with the help of many graduate and undergraduate students, is based on the premise that a carefully and thoughtfully designed family literacy program could serve two purposes: it could teach "the codes needed to participate fully in the mainstream of American life" (Delpit, 1995 p. 45) and, at the same time, could uncover, recognize, and build on the household funds of knowledge described by Moll and his colleagues (Diaz, Moll, & Mehan, 1986; Gonzalez et al., 1995; Moll & Greenberg, 1991). As such, I believed that the family literacy program could open doors and opportunities for parents and children, ultimately leading to learning success for both generations, and open minds of teachers to the rich and diverse resources families offer to their own children and, with encouragement, might offer to the larger learning community. During the last ten years, the Intergenerational Literacy Project (ILP) has served more than 1,300 families, most of whom were new immigrants who journeyed to the United States from 43 different countries. In the chapter that follows, I provide a detailed description of how the program came to be.

CHAPTER

2

The Intergenerational Literacy Project

The Intergenerational Literacy Project (ILP) was begun in 1989 to achieve three purposes:

- To improve the English literacy of parents
- To support the literacy development and academic success of their children
- To conduct research on the effectiveness of an intergenerational approach to literacy

To accomplish these goals, the ILP offers literacy instruction to parents of preschool and school-age children. No direct instruction is provided to children; rather, the project is based on the premise that as parents improve their own literacy, the skills and knowledge they gain will promote literacy learning among their children. In addition, as parents share reading and writing with their children, they will support their own literacy learning through practice and application.

In this chapter, I describe the community in which the ILP is situated, the educational principles that guided its planning and implementation, and the practices that were derived based on the educational principles.

The Community

The Intergenerational Literacy Project was implemented in the community of Chelsea, Massachusetts, a small, densely populated city of approximately 35,000 people living within two square miles. In 1986, the mayor of Chelsea, John Brennan, and the school committee chairman, Andrew Quigley, approached Boston University President John Silber with a request that Boston University study the schools' problems and recommend solutions. Over a ten-month period, a comprehensive evaluation was carried out and a report of the findings and a plan of action were presented to the city of Chelsea and the Chelsea School Committee. After much public debate about the wisdom of the reform effort, the Chelsea School Committee and the Board of Aldermen asked the Massachusetts Legislature to approve a home-rule bill that would permit Boston University to assume the management of the schools for a period of ten years. The legislature approved the historic school reform effort and established an oversight panel to conduct annual reviews of the partnership. As stipulated by the agreement, the university's responsibilities were to hire the superintendent; enter into collective bargaining agreements; set curriculum, instruction, and personnel policies; formulate the annual budget and oversee expenditures; and seek external funds. The school committee was afforded the right to review all activities and issues and to request reconsideration, overrule the university by a two-thirds vote on all matters except personnel matters, and end the ten-year contract and dismiss the university at any time by a simple majority vote. The goals of the partnership were summarized around three simple principles: (1) something important must be taught, (2) children must be ready to learn, and (3) teachers must be ready to teach (Greenes, 1994).

In an article detailing the history of the partnership, Greenes (1994) provided the following portrait of the community as this work began:

> Over the past century, Chelsea has seen successive waves of immigrants: Irish, Italians, Eastern Europeans, Puerto Ricans, Central Americans, and Southeast Asians. At one time a city flourishing with activity and known for its outstanding school system, Chelsea is now beset by poverty, racial unrest, and substance abuse problems. Streets are lined with cramped brick tenements and wooden triple-deckers. Factories and oil tanks block access to the harbor. A giant toll bridge looms above the city. Lead-paint chips from the bridge contaminate the soil, and exhaust fumes pollute the air. A great many of the city's homes and businesses were burned in the fire of 1973 and were never replaced. Employers who once hired large numbers of unskilled workers have left the city.
>
> For the twenty years prior to 1989, the Chelsea public schools had not met all the needs of the 3500 children. The schools had the state's highest high school dropout rate and the lowest student SAT scores. School buildings were old and in disrepair. (p. 9)

Throughout its history, Chelsea has served as a gateway to the United States for several new waves of immigrants; as a result, its demographics are ever-changing: 28 percent of the families presently living in Chelsea arrived in the community from other countries after 1980. Census data from 1990 indicated that the population of the community was 59 percent White, 31 percent Hispanic, 5 percent Asian or Pacific Islander, 4 percent African American, and 1 percent other.

Chelsea is a community growing in size as well. Since 1980, its population has grown by 25 percent. Chelsea remains a poor community, with a quarter of its population living below the poverty level. The most recently reported unemployment rate of 6.7 percent is approximately double the reported statewide rate of 3 percent. Approximately 60 percent of the adult community has achieved a higher school diploma or higher.

At the present time, the school has approximately 5,400 students in kindergarten to grade 12. The large majority of children attending the public schools are children of color. Most recent data indicate that approximately 65 percent of schoolchildren are Hispanic, 18 percent are White, 9 percent are African American, and 8 percent are Asian. Seventy-three percent of the students speak a first language other than English. Nearly 12 percent of children between the ages of 3 and 21 have attended American schools for fewer than three years. Seventy-three percent of the students are eligible for free and reduced-price lunch programs. The annual dropout rate is approximately 13 percent, compared to a statewide average of just above 3 percent.

The early years of the Boston University–Chelsea School Partnership were contentious. As described by Sears (1994) five years into the agreement:

> The Boston University/Chelsea Partnership was initiated in an atmosphere of distrust. The constitutionality of the Partnership was challenged by the teachers' union and a group of Chelsea residents. Skepticism remains, but in 1994 professional relationships among those working in the schools—from Boston University and from Chelsea—are strong. Public meetings are significantly less contentious. More importantly, the close and enduring working relationships between Chelsea teachers and administrators and their colleagues from Boston University have provided a sturdy foundation on which sound curriculum and excellent teaching are being built. (p. 21-22)

After the first ten years of school reform, there were several indications that the reform effort was making a difference. A report of the partnership to the legislature noted that the average score of third-grade students taking the Iowa Test of Basic Skills increased by 11 percentile points from 1998 to 1999, more than twice the average gain statewide; Scholastic Aptitude Test (SAT) results for Chelsea High school had increased, even as the numbers of students taking the test also increased; attendance rates were up, particularly among high school students; and, in an independent study of school districts that had significantly exceeded projections of expected academic achievement based on the districts demography, the Chelsea schools were judged as "noteworthy" (Gaudet, 2000).

In 1998, as the initial contract period neared completion, the school committee, with full support from members of the community, voted to extend the university's leadership for an additional five-year period.

Guiding Educational Principles

The Boston University–Chelsea School Partnership was initiated in a climate in which parents were perceived to be at least partially to blame for the decline of the schools. Describing his vision for the Partnership, John Silber (1994) wrote:

> In the heydey of the public schools, students typically came home from two-parent families, the father a breadwinner and the mother a homemaker. A grandparent or unmarried aunt or uncle might also be a member of the household.
>
> The adults in these households were often poorly educated themselves, but they respected learning and the discipline necessary for success in school and beyond. Thus the sons and daughters of immigrants (and native-born Americans) learned while still very young that education was the key to making it in America, a lesson that was continually reinforced by parents who took a keen interest in their children's education, who made sure their children did their homework, who got to know their children's teachers and worked with those teachers to ensure their children's success in school. These children came to school prepared to learn.

Too few children in America, wherever they are born, are taught such lessons in the home. That sort of family is now the exception, not the rule. In many households today, there is only one adult, usually a single mother who is perhaps ill equipped to deal with the responsibilities and unable to pay close attention to her child's education. She may be only a child herself, and hers is thus a no-parent family.

And even if there are two parents at home, both are likely to be working outside the home, making it difficult for either to become adequately involved in their children's education. All too often, television becomes the substitute for conversation with adults and for more enriching forms of recreations. These children arrive at school already at a deficit. (p. 4)

Claims such as these heightened tension in the community and were often met with rhetoric that was negative and politically charged. The spotlight that had been shone on the schools and the community was virtually impossible to escape, and despite the often negative tone that accompanied public speech, the partnership generated high levels of energy, excitement, and interest and a clear commitment to education among many teachers and parents. These latter characteristics set the stage for the successful implementation of the ILP.

With a substantial, three-year grant from the U.S. Department of Education's FIRST Initiative and smaller awards from the Massachusetts Department of Education and a few private foundations,[1] the Intergenerational Literacy Project became one of the very first initiatives of the larger school reform effort. Its purpose was to improve the English literacy and language of adults and to support parents in their efforts to help their children achieve school success. In addition, we hoped to use the project as a context for conducting research on the effectiveness of family literacy interventions. As we planned a project that would enable us to achieve these goals, several educational principles guided us.

1. Literacy is a sociocultural process. That is, it is the "ability of individuals to interpret and to act upon the world within cultural and social communities of practice" (Duran, 1996). As such, instructional contexts and activities that succeed in supporting literacy development of parents and their children must be both relevant and important in the lives of the participants.
2. An approach to literacy learning that emphasizes biliteracy and biculturalism "creates the expanded possibility of accessing funds of knowledge from the lived experiences of two or more social worlds" (Moll, 1998, p. 74).
3. Forming instructional groups that are heterogeneous with regard to first language, culture, and English language and literacy proficiency affords students the most effective learning climate. Further, classroom groups that emphasize cooperative learning and collaboration among students enhance their opportunities to learn.
4. Instruction that is cognitively oriented and framed by a strategic approach to reading and writing helps students to direct their own learning and to attribute success to themselves and their own efforts, rather than to their teachers, thus enabling them to continue to succeed after exiting from a structured learning program.

5. Programs that instruct parents in sharing storybooks with children introduce them, and subsequently their children, to a discourse that is important for children's success in early literacy.
6. The purpose of assessment is to inform instruction, thereby improving participants' opportunities to learn. As such, assessment must be situated within the context of tasks and texts that are relevant and important in the daily lives of learners and their children.

The following section presents a brief summary of the research and theory underlying each of these principles and the particular ways in which the principles influenced program planning and implementation.

Sociocultural Learning

In explaining his theory of learning, Vygotsky (1978) posited that the process of internalizing learning is one in which, first, an external activity is restructured and begins to occur internally, and second, an interpersonal process is transformed into an intrapersonal one—a series of steps in which every function appears twice: "first, on a social level, and later, on the individual level" (p. 57). Emphasizing the social nature of learning, Vygotsky reiterated: "All the higher functions originate as actual relations between human individuals" (p. 57).

Strongly influenced by Vygotskian theory, Moll (1992) argued that "a major role of schooling is to create social contexts for the mastery of and conscious awareness in the use of" (p. 213) tools that mediate learning. Moll described this approach to learning as sociocultural and explained that, as such, it examines "literacy in connection to the complex social relationships and cultural practices of human beings, be it in classrooms or in community settings" (p. 211). Applied specifically to family literacy intervention programs, Auerbach (1989) described a sociocultural approach as one in which

> Housing, work, and health issues are acknowledged and explored in the classroom, with literacy becoming a tool for addressing these issues, and cultural differences are perceived as strengths and resources that can bridge the gap between home and school. As these issues become part of the curriculum content, literacy will become more socially significant for families, which . . . is what characterizes the families of successful readers. (p. 176)

Duran (1996) argued that a sociocultural approach to literacy and language learning is especially important in settings in which participants are also acquiring a second language:

> Research suggests that learners of a second language acquire the second language most effectively when it arises as comprehensible input (i.e., when the use of the second language arises in authentic social contexts with extended meaning and uses for practical problem solving). (p. 26)

An understanding and conviction that literacy learning is a sociocultural process shaped the instructional routines that frame a typical project day at the ILP:

- Adults read and respond in small groups to literacy materials that address topics of interest in their own lives or in the lives of their children.
- Adults read and respond to literacy materials appropriate for sharing or use with their children in home settings.
- Adults are provided a forum for sharing their family literacy experiences with their friends and teachers.

In response to evidence that effective literacy instruction is situated within socially and culturally relevant contexts (e.g., Auerbach, 1989, 1992; Gee, 1999; Schieffelin & Cochran-Smith, 1984; Taylor, 1993), emphasis is placed on helping adults use literacy to mediate existing family routines, rather than on creating school-like literacy contexts in the home setting.

Curricular materials are those that are typically found in home or community settings. They include materials of particular interest to parents, such as oral histories, nutrition and child care information, books or articles about child development, and local and national newspapers and magazines. In addition, the curriculum includes a large collection of children's books, which are often read and discussed in class in preparation for reading at home with their children.

Biliterate and Bicultural Approach

Although research related to bilingual education has been marked by considerable controversy (Goldenberg, 1996; Moran & Hakuta, 1995; Weber, 1991), a few well-designed studies have yielded some important findings related to the influence of bilingualism on cognition. These studies have led several researchers (e.g., Diaz, 1983; Hakuta, 1986; Moran & Hakuta, 1995) to argue that bilinguals bring important cognitive strengths to the classroom that, when recognized and built on by knowledgeable teachers, provide students additional learning resources. In the context of the ILP, instructional emphasis on any particular language or culture is complicated by the multilingual, multicultural nature of the learning community. From the start, we recognized that the diversity of the participants we expected to serve and the large number of first languages spoken among them restricted us from offering a truly bilingual approach that provided balanced and explicit instruction in the learners' first languages and in English. Nonetheless, we were committed to recognizing and building on language and cultural differences as strengths. To do so, we adopted a structured immersion approach, defined by Weber (1991) as one in which "the general use of English [is] adjusted . . . along with assistance in the mother tongue at moments judged relevant by the teacher or aide" (p. 103). We chose English texts for classroom use but encouraged students to form "language-alike" groups to prepare to read and to respond to reading in the language of their choice. This approach is consistent with studies of effective classroom instruction for language minority students. In one study, for example, Garcia (1988) reported that across 58 classrooms identified as offering children effective instruction, English was used approximately 60 percent of the time and the first language or a combination of first and second languages was used the rest of the time. Garcia found noteworthy the particular way the two languages were combined:

> Successful teachers for LEP [limited English proficient] students mediated instruction for LEP students by the use of the student's native language (L1) and English (L2) for instruction, alternating between the two languages whenever necessary to ensure clarity of instruction. (p. 391)

According to Moll (1998), this biliterate–bicultural approach to learning serves an important "amplifying" function:

> It allows teachers and students access to literate resources in two languages. These literate resources allow students to access knowledge and experiences that may not be found in their immediate community. But this connection can also be mediated. For example, students can learn how to relate experiences from their communities to issues or problems found in the literature, or use the knowledge from the literature to rethink issues in the community, thus providing options for thinking that may otherwise not exist. (p. 74)

To facilitate the implementation of this approach, we staffed each class of 25 adult learners with a team of two teachers and three tutors. The two teachers were graduate students, primarily in education, and the three tutors were undergraduate students in any college or school within Boston University. We sought to have every member of the teaching team bilingual and to have at least one person on each team fluent in one of the languages spoken by the learners in the class.

Cooperative Grouping

As we considered how to assign adults to classes, we reviewed research related to grouping practices and literacy learning. In the absence of studies that focused particularly on grouping practices in adult education, we relied on evidence from investigations related to the teaching of reading in elementary and secondary schooling. Drawing from several research syntheses and related studies of ability grouping, we reached two conclusions that were highly influential in shaping the ILP. First, with few exceptions, investigations indicated that grouping students by reading proficiency levels did not lead to higher levels of achievement and often had particularly negative consequences for students who were placed in the lowest achievement groups (e.g., Good & Marshall, 1984; Hiebert, 1983; Oakes, 1985; Slavin, 1987). Second, evidence indicated that students placed in low-achieving groups often experience low self-esteem and negative attitudes toward reading and learning (Dweck, 1986; Eder, 1983; Swanson, 1985).

In addition, we reviewed investigations of heterogeneous grouping, with particular emphasis on cooperative grouping (e.g., Johnson, Maruyama, Johnson, & Nelson, 1981; Sharan, 1980; Slavin, 1980). In addition to the evidence that students of all ability levels who work in cooperative learning groups do better than their peers who work in traditional groups, there was a second finding that held particular importance for the linguistically and culturally diverse community where the ILP was situated. Investigations indicated that students who work in cooperative learning groups have an opportunity to develop strong interpersonal ties and a better understanding of how to develop social relationships. We believed that the literacy classes should provide a context in which adults could explore and learn about the cultural and linguistic differences among them and build strong interpersonal ties within their own communities. Forming groups based on either English-language proficiency or English-literacy proficiency would likely lead to groups segregated by language and would prevent the "multiracial community building" (Orfield & Yun, 1999) that we hoped to accomplish.

In response to the data related to grouping, we developed a grouping model based on the premise of flexible grouping (Radencich & McKay, 1995), an organizational framework that relies on strategic use of a range of grouping options throughout the literacy instructional period. The full range of grouping options includes whole-class instruction, generally used to introduce ideas, concepts, skills, or strategies that are new to all or almost all of the students in a classroom; teacher- or tutor-led homogeneous groups for instruction, review, or additional practice of information needed by particular learners; student-led heterogeneous groups for practice and application of previously taught information or for response groups; and individual response, also for practice and application of previously taught information or for written response.

The flexible grouping model implemented in the ILP is based on a model originally developed for use in elementary school classrooms (Paratore, 1991; Radencich et al., 1995). It is intended to create a context that supports the development of the classroom as a learning community, where a focus on the same text or topic enables learners to interact and provides an opportunity for them to learn from one another. Within the cooperative groups that mark the reading and response segments of the literacy lessons, we emphasize a practice that Tharp and Gallimore (1988) termed "instructional conversation," later defined by Goldenberg 1992–93) as "discussion-based lessons geared toward creating richly textured opportunities for students' conceptual and linguistic development" (p. 317). Jiménez and Gersten (1999) contrasted the instructional conversation with traditional recitation patterns in which teachers engage students in simple question–response patterns:

> The instructional conversation differs in that a key goal is to elicit more extended discourse from students, often on a specified theme, while intermittently providing necessary background information. The teacher encourages and promotes an overall accepting and nonthreatening atmosphere within which the conversation takes place. This approach aims for conversations designed to promote learning. (p. 277)

Strategic Reading

Paris, Wasik, and Turner (1991) defined reading strategies as "actions selected deliberately to achieve particular goals" (p. 611). In contrast to reading skills, which are "applied to text unconsciously for many reasons including expertise, repeated practice, compliance with directions, luck, and naïve use," reading strategies are "conscious and deliberate . . . they can be evaluated for their utility, effort, and appropriateness" (Paris et al., 1991, p. 611). In their review of research related to strategic reading, Paris et al. (1991) explained the importance of a strategic approach:

> First, strategies allow readers to elaborate, organize, and evaluate information derived from text. Second, the acquisition of reading strategies coincides and overlaps with the development . . . of multiple cognitive strategies to enhance attention, memory, communication, and learning. Third, strategies are controllable by readers; they are personal cognitive tools that can be used selectively and flexibly. Fourth, strategic reading reflects metacognition and motivation because readers need to have both the knowledge and disposition to use strategies. Fifth, strategies that foster reading and thinking can be taught directly by teachers. And sixth, strategic reading can enhance learning throughout the curriculum. (p. 609)

Becoming a strategic reader has been integrally connected to the development of metacognitive abilities. Cognitive and metacognitive theorists explain that metacognitive knowledge is acquired in two stages: recognition, that is, awareness that something is difficult, unclear, or confusing; and regulation, that is, knowing how to resolve the difficulty or problem (Brown, Armbruster, & Baker, 1986; Flavell, 1979). Further, researchers suggest that regulation is multifaceted, requiring awareness of many factors, including knowledge of text (e.g., "this is hard for me because it's nonfiction, and I don't like nonfiction"), knowledge of an appropriate learning strategy ("if I make a map of the important ideas, I will understand better"), and accurate assessment of the match between the task and knowledge of the strategy ("even though this is difficult, I know this strategy will help me"). (See, for example, Brown et al., 1986; Flavell & Wellman, 1977; Palmer & Goetz, 1988.)

Recent investigations have provided evidence that comprehension can be improved through explicit teaching of "repertoires of comprehension strategies" (Pressley, 1998) that provide students with procedures for monitoring and regulating their attention and response to text before, during, and after reading. Defined by many as "cognitively-oriented instruction" (e.g., Jiménez & Gersten, 1999), this model incorporates three fundamental teaching practices: the use of think-alouds or "mental modeling" to demonstrate the use of a particular reading strategy, the use of graphic organizers and visual displays to organize information and to represent the relationships between and among ideas, and frequent and ongoing feedback to learners, articulating how well they are acquiring and applying strategies that have been taught. Throughout the course of instruction, emphasis is placed on helping learners to attribute success to themselves and their own efforts, rather than to their teachers, enabling them to continue to succeed after exiting from this particular program.

Shared Storybook Reading

For years, studies have reported a positive correlation between children's reading success and their preschool experiences. Beginning as early as 1908, Edmund Huey called attention to the role parents play in children's beginning reading, explaining:

Almost as naturally as the sun shines, in those sittings on the parent's knee, [the child] comes to feel and to say the right parts of the story or rhyme as his eye and finger travel over the printed lines. . . . The secret of it all lies in parents' reading aloud to and with the child. (p. 332)

Later, the work of Dolores Durkin (1966) came to be viewed as essential in helping us understand the roles parents play in children's reading success. In two investigations in which she compared the home experiences of early and nonearly readers, Durkin found that early readers had parents who spent time with their children, who read to them, who answered their questions and their requests for help, and who demonstrated in their own lives that reading is a rich source of relaxation, information, and commitment. She concluded that:

early readers are not a special brand of children who can be readily identified and sorted by tests. Rather, it would seem, it is their mothers who play the key role in effecting the early achievement. The homes they provide, the example they show, the time they give to the children, their concepts of their role as educator of the preschool child—all of these dimensions of home life and of parent–child relationships appeared to be of singular importance to the early reading achievement described in this report. (p. 138)

Ten years later, Marie Clark (1976) reported similar findings in her study of young fluent readers:

A number of the fluent readers had available an interested adult with time to devote to them at the stage when they were interested in reading—either to read to them, talk with them, or answer their questions. (p. 102)

Over time, findings from studies such as these received widespread support from many other investigations (e.g., Briggs & Elkind, 1977; Dunn, 1981; Mason, 1980; Morrow, 1983). In 1985, the Commission on Reading, charged by the National Academy of Education's Commission on Education and Public Policy to "locate topics on which there has been appreciable research and scholarship . . . to survey, interpret and synthesize research findings" (Anderson, Hiebert, Scott, & Wilkinson, 1985, p. viii), underscored the importance of shared storybook reading in their conclusion that "the single most important activity for building the knowledge required for eventual success in reading is reading aloud to children" (p. 23).

Although some (e.g., Scarborough & Dobrich, 1994) have argued that the relationship between storybook reading and children's early reading success may be more moderate than it is generally believed to be, others stand by the conclusion that the relationship is strong. A meta-analysis conducted by Bus, van Ijzendoorn, and Pellegrini (1995) of 29 related studies led them to conclude that the data "support the assumption that parent-preschooler reading is a *necessary* preparation for beginning reading instruction" (p. 17, emphasis added).

Finally, in her study of the home literacy experiences of children in 20 low-income families, Purcell-Gates (1996) attempted to sort out whether it was experience with print generally, or storybook reading in particular, that influenced children's preparation for school. She reported that although "the families in the study all used print for various purposes as they went about their daily activities and pursuits" (p. 425), children who had experiences with the types of written discourse found in storybooks, novels, magazine articles, and newspapers begin school with "schemata for literacy which puts them at an advantage over their peers" (p. 426) who have not had these types of experiences.

Some have criticized the work connecting storybook reading and successful school achievement as correlational and, as such, inconclusive. For example, Arnold and Whitehurst (1994) argue that engagement in shared storybook reading may be only one very evident sign of a range of many other equally important, but less visible, parental values:

> Though it is easy to imagine that reading picture books at home and in day care or preschool directly prepares children for the demands of formal reading, it is also easy to imagine that shared picture book reading at home is simply a marker of parental values. Homes in which books are provided for young children and in which shared reading occurs frequently are also likely to be homes in which parents value education, read frequently themselves, use sophisticated vocabulary, and provide other forms of intellectual stimulation for children. (p. 12)

However, the argument that shared reading is nothing more than a "marker" for a constellation of other activities that support children's school success is refuted by the evidence (presented in Chapter 1) that absence of family storybook reading cannot be taken as indication of lack of parental values for education, impoverished language use, or limited intellectual or cognitive stimulation (e.g., Delgado-Gaitan, 1990, 1992; Moll, Amanti, Neff, & Gonzalez, 1992; Taylor & Dorsey-Gaines, 1988; Valdés, 1996). Rather, it seems that the high degree of congruence between the oral and written discourse experiences provided by shared storybook reading and the tasks required of children in kindergarten and first-grade literacy lessons explains the apparent power of storybook reading in preparing children for reading success.

In sum, the evidence related to family storybook reading suggests that despite the presence of many rich and important family literacy practices, unfamiliarity with storybook reading disadvantages children in the early stages of learning to read. Therefore, although it is important to help teachers learn to acknowledge and build on the literacies children bring to school, it is also important to introduce parents to reading and writing practices that will effectively prepare their children for early literacy classrooms. In the ILP, we view introducing parents to effective strategies for shared storybook reading as one component of this responsibility. In addition to being introduced to specific books to read with their children, parents are taught how to ask questions about the selection, how to encourage their children to ask questions, and how to engage their children in response to books. As well, parents are taught how to encourage children's writing, including invented spellings, how to help schoolage children with homework, the types of questions they might ask their children about the school day, and the types of questions they might ask the classroom teacher to find out about their children's progress.

Authentic Assessment

The Literacy Dictionary (Harris & Hodges, 1995) defines assessment as:

> The act or process of gathering data in order to better understand the strengths and weaknesses of student learning, as by observation, testing, interviews etc. (p. 12)

Beyond a simple definition of *assessment*, experts also have explored the factors that influence the accuracy and trustworthiness of data that are collected. Archbald and Newmann (1988), for example, argued that to collect evidence that is an accurate reflection of what learners truly know and do, assessment must be conducted in a context that is *authentic*. They described authentic assessment as having three essential traits: it engages students in tasks that approximate those that experts perform, it requires students to join the pieces of a project into an integrated whole, and it has utility beyond evaluation.

Chittenden (1991) elaborated on this definition by comparing authentic assessment with traditional assessment. In contrast to short-answer or multiple-choice response formats, authentic assessment is open-ended; instead of decontextualized formal assessment tasks, authentic assessment is based on work samples drawn from ongoing instructional tasks; instead of independent, "teacher-proof" assigned tasks, authentic assessment may be teacher-mediated; instead of annual or periodic, scheduled evaluation periods, authentic assessment is ongoing and cumulative.

As we engaged in the initial planning of the ILP, our purpose was to adhere to the tenets of authentic assessment and collect data within contexts that were important and relevant to the lives of the families we served. By so doing, we expected to collect data that would allow us to effectively inform and plan instruction on an ongoing basis. Because the ILP offers service directly to parents and, through them, to their children, we sought to monitor the literacy learning of the adults participating in the project and to monitor the influence of project instruction and activities on the ways they shared literacy with their children at home. To achieve these purposes, we implemented a portfolio approach to assessment (Tierney, Carter, & Desai, 1991; Wolf, 1989), which included literacy logs detailing daily uses of literacy at home alone and with their children, daily writing samples, and periodic running records of oral reading. In addition to the portfolio data, we conducted intake and exit interviews with each parent, and we monitored and recorded daily attendance.

The Principles in Action

With the aforementioned principles as our foundation, we set about the process of implementing the program. This process included developing community relationships, recruiting families, securing a site, providing instruction, and monitoring learning. This section describes each of these steps.

Developing Community Relationships

As we planned the ILP, we gave careful thought to the particular services we would offer and considered the range of services that the families we hoped to serve would likely need. We expected that many of the families would confront obstacles in their daily lives such as housing, health, and employment. We were committed to creating a learning context in which parents could learn to use literacy actions and interactions to assist in their mediation of the many difficult circumstances in their daily lives. At the same time, we were aware that satisfactory resolution of many of the challenges they faced would require collaboration with a variety of human resource agencies within the community. As noted previously, however, the Boston University–Chelsea School Partnership began in a climate of distrust and skepticism, and among those most suspicious of the university's motives and intentions were community-based, human resource organizations that depended on competitive funding to maintain their own programs and services. Many among them worried that the university's reputation and high profile would make it difficult, if not impossible, for them to compete for pools of money of common interest. We believed that the level of concern and distrust held by many of the agencies toward the university would influence the extent to which we could work collaboratively and effectively to meet the needs of the families whose interests we held in common. Therefore, as the first step in preparing for implementation of the family literacy program, we sought to establish a foundation for trust and collaboration within the community. We began by arranging a meeting with members of the Literacy Coalition, a local group that represented existing adult and child literacy programs in the community and numerous other agencies, including health, public welfare, housing, and alternative education programs. At the meeting, we described the family literacy program as it was currently envisioned and sought feedback and advice from coalition members. We pledged that we would not move ahead with our plans until members of the coalition were satisfied that the services we intended to offer would not duplicate existing services and therefore would not compete for funding with them. Achieving this goal turned out to be a lengthy process, requiring many hours of individual meetings with program directors and group meetings with the coalition. After approximately six months, we finally reached agreement and won the coalition's support. The Intergenerational Literacy Project was launched with a long list of collaborators committed to helping it succeed, including the directors of the elementary school Title 1 program, the community adult education program, and the community alternative education and parenting teen programs; representatives from the Department of Public Welfare, Human Services Collaborative, and Bilingual Parents Advisory Council; and clergy from the faith-based groups in the community.

In the early stages of project implementation, members of the coalition assisted by identifying and recruiting parents who were particularly well-suited to an intergenerational literacy project; helping to locate space within the community where classes could be held; identifying teachers who would have particular interest in the program; and identifying potential funding sources. As the ILP became an established program in the community, we were able to reciprocate by referring learners to programs within the community that were suited to their individual needs and by working together to offer families the full range of services they needed in the course of their daily lives.

Recruiting Families

We used several strategies to inform community members of the new project and to recruit families. We met with community leaders and neighborhood organizations. We spoke with school professionals, particularly those who worked closely with parents, such as school counselors, reading teachers, and classroom teachers. We distributed flyers (in four different languages) by posting them in neighborhood stores, community centers, and public places and by sending them home with schoolchildren. We posted announcements on local television and radio stations. Our experiences during recruitment led us to draw some important conclusions about the process. First, involving community agencies is a critical step in achieving widespread interest and participation. Although elementary and secondary teachers were supportive in distributing program information, it was the community leaders who helped us reach parents during the initial stages of the project. Project staff visited and called community leaders frequently; they brought program information to meetings with staff and parents at various agencies. Of particular help in recruiting families were clergy, leaders of bilingual and cultural organizations, and health professionals. Announcements were made at church services and community center meetings. Community leaders reviewed written notices and helped develop accurate translations for bilingual parents. They also distributed information by including notices in church bulletins and posting them in community centers and neighborhood stores. Many community leaders contacted parents directly to describe the project and to ask if they would like to participate.

After the initial start-up, the recruiting process changed. Our best recruiters became the parents who participated. Classes grew as parents brought their friends and family members. In several cases, we have enrolled the mother, the father, and a grandparent from a single family. Although we still print program brochures so that we can distribute them to teachers and community leaders for them to give to particular families, we no longer conduct long-scale distribution efforts. Our classes are continually full, and we maintain a long waiting list most of the time.

We learned, however, that building stable enrollment takes time. It took several weeks and a great deal of networking to recruit the first 16 families, and then several more weeks and meetings with community leaders to build beyond that initial enrollment. By the third year, we were serving more than 75 families in each cycle, with many more on a waiting list. Program administrators who expect or demand quick enrollment may be disappointed with the results.

Securing a Site

During its ten-year history, the ILP has occupied many different locations. In the first three years, we rented space in a local community center for morning classes. Not designed as classroom space, these rooms were clean and spacious but lacked the instructional apparatus—such as chalkboards, bookshelves, and round tables for discussion groups—beneficial to learning. By the end of the third year, the program had grown in popularity in the community, and consequently the school administration viewed it as an important program. As a result, during the fourth and fifth years of the program, classrooms in one of the elementary school buildings were allocated for ILP use. Located on the same corridor where many of the parents' children attended classes, these classrooms provided excellent learning space and wonderful opportunities for collaborating with elementary teachers. However, as the elementary school enrollment grew, the classrooms that had been allocated to the ILP were reassigned to children, and the ILP was again relocated, this time to a building in the community where space was renovated for the ILP and another adult education program. Although this was excellent instructional space, its location several blocks from any of the elementary schools made it difficult to establish ongoing collaboration between ILP teachers and elementary teachers or between ILP parents and teachers. Within just three years of this relocation, the school system built all new schools, and the ILP was provided space within the new Early Learning Center. However, shortly after moving in, the burgeoning school population again resulted in a change in space, and in the reduction of two classrooms. The remaining classroom was divided in two by a partition to accommodate two classes, and the third was assigned to space in a large and open lobby area.

So, what have we learned from this location–relocation history? First, in this climate of growing enrollments, school officials were dedicated to providing instructional services to children before other priorities, and this meant that all other programs were viewed as optional. It is difficult to fault this stance, but it certainly created a challenge to effective implementation of the ILP. We met it by maintaining a belief that, in the final analysis, the quality of teaching outweighs any other programmatic feature (Chall & Feldman, 1966; Fisher et al., 1978; Venezky & Winfield, 1979). Thus, in the face of frequently changing classroom space, we rigidly adhered to the educational principles previously outlined.

Second, we reject the widely held assumption that adults are intimidated by public school settings and that, consequently, programs that focus on adult learning are more appropriately held in community settings. Instead, we have found public school settings to be effective contexts for adult literacy classes. Location in these settings has allowed several special projects, including parents as classroom storybook readers, as literacy tutors, and as reading partners. In one school, parents chose to become library aides, and they helped children select and check out books and conduct story hours during library visits. Such experiences have permitted parents to become important members of the school's literacy community, and they also have provided them with authentic contexts for practicing their own literacy. Further, being present on nearly a daily basis in their children's schools has helped parents understand the differences in the norms for appropriate communication at home and at school. They have developed an understanding of what Corno (1989) referred to as "classroom literacy"—an understanding of how classrooms work.

Providing Instruction

Instruction is planned to achieve a twofold purpose: (1) to provide parents an opportunity to read and respond to materials of adult interest and (2) to provide a selection of books, strategies, and ideas for use with their children. Adults may attend literacy classes either mornings or evenings. Morning classes are offered four days per week, two hours per session, and child care is offered for preschool-age children. Evening classes are offered three days per week, two hours per session, and child care is offered for both preschool and schoolage children.

Instruction is organized within 15-week instructional cycles. Classes are 25 adults who are heterogeneous in relation to first languages, home cultures, and English literacy and language proficiencies. They are taught by a team of five people: two certified and experienced literacy teachers and three tutors. The teachers are graduate students at Boston University; the tutors are undergraduate students, also at Boston University. The tutors attend a weekly tutoring seminar taught by the project teachers. Each 15-week cycle concludes with an award ceremony, at which learners receive a certificate marking their participation for a full cycle.

Over the course of each week, approximately half of class time is devoted to reading and writing materials of adult interest and to developing specific skills to extend their own literacy abilities, and half the time is spent becoming familiar with materials and strategies for supporting their children's literacy learning. Each day's activities are planned in accordance with the six educational principles presented in brief in Figure 2.1 and elaborated on in the earlier section.

FIGURE 2.1   Guiding Educational Principles

Guiding Educational Principles

1. Literacy is a sociocultural process. As such, instructional conversations that build on learners' knowledge of each other and their communities and their shared understanding of the texts they are reading dominate classroom discourse.
2. Instruction builds upon the biliterate and bicultural backgrounds of the learners and teachers.
3. Classes are heterogeneous with regard to first language, culture, and English language and literacy proficiency. Within classes, small, cooperative groups that are alike in language and literacy proficiencies may be formed during the course of a lesson.
4. Instruction is cognitively oriented in nature and framed by a strategic approach to reading and writing.
5. Instruction in sharing storybooks with children is a central part of routine instruction.
6. Assessment is ongoing and is situated within the context of tasks and texts that are relevent and important in the daily lives of learners and their children.

Although each classroom and each day varies according to individual differences among teachers and the particular learners they serve, in general, daily activities are framed as follows.

Supporting family literacy. Each day, parents make an entry on a two-sided literacy log. On one side, they record and comment on the literacy events or activities in which they engaged with their child on the previous day. On the other side of the log, they record and comment on the literacy events or activities in which they engaged alone. At the beginning of the instructional cycle, a brief discussion typically precedes completion of the logs. Learners are asked many questions by the teachers and tutors: What literacy events did they share with their child? Who initiated it? Why? Did it connect to something else? Did the child like it? How did they know? Did they like it? Why or why not? After writing, parents share their log entries with a small group. Often, this sharing results in exchanging and even reading all or parts of favorite children's storybooks.

As previously noted, an essential goal of the ILP is to influence the practice of family literacy. Toward that end, the literacy log serves a dual purpose. First, by requiring parents to report each day on their previous day's home literacy experiences, we raise their awareness of the ways they use literacy in their daily lives. With increased awareness, we hope to promote increased regulation. Further, as we discuss entries with parents, we sometimes learn that they have interpreted our encouragement to engage in family literacy as a push toward school-like literacies, and parents report routine use of workbook and other decontextualized, school-like tasks. The sharing and discussion that emerge from the literacy log entries enable us to emphasize the importance of initiating family literacy events and practices that are important and relevant in the daily lives of children and adults, rather than those that duplicate tasks children may be required to do in school. Second, the logs also serve a documentation function by providing a record of routine uses of literacy in families throughout their period of participation. Although as self-reported data the logs lack the rigor of information collected more objectively, they nonetheless provide some evidence of what parents viewed as worthy of doing and reporting throughout their period of participation. Figure 2.2 provides an example of a completed literacy log.

Supporting adult literacy through reading lessons. To accommodate the heterogeneous nature of the class, a flexible grouping model frames the daily reading lesson. The focal texts are often chosen collaboratively by teachers and learners and thus vary from classroom to classroom and from cycle to cycle. They are selected from materials that are typically found in home or community settings and include texts that have particular relevance and importance in the lives of the learners and their children. Commonly used texts include articles from the local newspapers to which each class subscribes; magazines, including *Parent and Child Magazine,* to which we have a subscription for every family; and *PBS Families,* a monthly guide to public television programming for children, which we receive in both English and Spanish. We often choose from brochures or announcements distributed by school officials and teachers or by community agencies, and we have found short stories addressing issues of

FIGURE 2.2   Sample Completed Literacy Log

Intergenerational Literacy Project
Boston University/Chelsea Public Schools

LITERACY LOG

NAME: _Lucy_

MONTH: _September 27-1995_

DATE	Reading, Writing, Viewing and Talking Activities of <u>Personal Interest</u>
9-20-95	I wrote a letter To my son in Dorchester yesterday.
9-21-95	yesterday I Called my friend on The phone.
9-25-95	Yesterday I read Some word about movies and the Television.
9-25-95	
9-27-95	yesterday my son Called me from his work.
11-7-95	Last night I wrote a letter to my son for Dorchester. Also I wrote a letter to my mother for Philadelfia.
11-16-95	Yesterday my friend colled me.
12-4-95	El sabado mi hijo vino a visitarme se llama Jorgi y esta en un programa de recuperacion por 9 meses.
12/6/95	Yesterday, I to look for different word in the dictionary.

Intergenerational Literacy Project
Boston University/Chelsea Public Schools

LITERACY LOG

NAME: _Lucy_

MONTH: _September 19, 1995_

DATE	Reading, Writing, Viewing and Talking Activities I Shared with My Child or Children	CHILD'S NAME AND AGE
9-19-95		·D'Engel
9-21-95	yesterday I wrote a note for my son to explain that I went to an appoinment.	
9-25-95	yesterday I read a letter from my son. With Dee.	
9-16-95	yesterday I helped my chid with a Homework of English.	
9-27-95	mañana 11 de Noviembre mi hijo D'Engel cumple 11 años y yo cumpro 1 año de estar en este programa estoy muy alegre porque como adulta nunca abia estado este tienpo estudiando.	

language and culture to be of high interest to participants. Of particular interest are personal narratives written by current and former ILP parents and available in the classroom in bound anthologies. Job applications, bills, and advertisements are also commonly used. In addition, the reading curriculum includes a large collection of children's books, many of which are read and discussed in class in preparation for reading at home with their children.

As indicated in Figure 2.3, reading activities are clustered around three major tasks: preparing to read, reading the selection, and responding to reading.

Preparing to read.   At the start of the literacy lesson, parents first meet as a whole class. At this time, a teacher or tutor distributes and introduces the day's focal text and elicits or builds important and relevant background knowledge. As learners preview the text, they contribute their ideas in the language of their choice, and teachers and tutors restate comments in English for the benefit of all participants. Vocabulary or concepts that may be unfamiliar to participants may be introduced at this time.

In addition, a reading strategy that will be especially useful in reading and understanding the particular text is either introduced or reviewed. Commonly used strategies include the use of prediction as a means of focusing attention and setting purpose,

FIGURE 2.3   Flexible Grouping and Instructional Framework for Reading Lessons

FLEXIBLE GROUPING AND INSTRUCTIONAL FRAMEWORK FOR LITERACY LESSONS

PREPARING TO READ
(Whole Class)

Accessing and building background knowledge
Asking questions
Introducing critical vocabulary
Selecting a reading strategy

READING THE SELECTION
(Small, Homogeneous Groups)

Reading the selection chorally, with partners, or individually
Discussing the selection

RESPONDING TO THE SELECTION
(Whole Class or Small, Heterogeneous Groups)

Retelling or summarizing the selection
Comparing to personal experiences and circumstances and to previous texts
Writing about the selection

graphic organizers to attend to text structure and discern relationships in text, and question generation and summarizing as ways to check and clarify understanding. Strategy instruction is explicit, guided by the work of Paris, Lipson, and Wixson (1983), who explained that explicit instruction requires not only telling students what they will be learning but also articulating the procedural and conditional knowledge they will need to successfully acquire and implement a strategy. As explained by Paris et al., procedural knowledge addresses *how* to use a strategy, the particular steps to be followed. Conditional knowledge includes the circumstances and purposes for initiating the particular strategy, when and why it would be beneficial or useful to the learners. Strategy instruction is also collaborative between the teacher and the learners, and in this aspect instruction is guided particularly by the model of gradual release of responsibility proposed by Pearson and Gallagher (1983), in which teachers initially accept responsibility to fully demonstrate and model a strategy, articulating what they are doing, how they are doing it, and why it is helpful. They then guide learners in the same process, following the Vygotskian (1978) model of providing expert assistance in a task that learners would likely be unable to accomplish on their own. Finally, over time, they observe students in their independent application of the strategy, monitor their performance, and intervene as appropriate.

Reading the selection. Learners convene in small groups formed on the basis of language and literacy proficiencies. Present in each group is a teacher or tutor; in most cases, though not all, this person has some degree of fluency in the first language of the group. Within these groups, learners read the text individually, in pairs, or with assistance from a teacher or tutor. They are also guided in the use of a reading strategy that is appropriate for the particular reading. Here, again, teachers and tutors are guided by a Vygotskian (1978) perspective. Working with individuals or in small groups, they provide as much assistance as a learner requires to successfully accomplish the task. After reading, learners, teachers, and tutors discuss the text among them and relate it to their own knowledge and experiences.

Responding to the selection. For this part of the lesson, the class may reconvene as a whole or in small, heterogeneous groups to share ideas, questions, and responses to the text. This part of the lesson is particularly influenced by the principles of the instructional conversation (Tharp & Gallimore, 1988). Goldenberg (1992–93) explained that the instructional conversation is characterized by five instructional elements (thematic focus, activation and use of background knowledge, direct teaching of a skill or concept by the teacher, promotion of more complex language and expression, and elicitation of bases for statements or positions) and five conversational elements (fewer known-answer questions, responsivity to student contributions, connected discourse, a challenging but nonthreatening atmosphere, and general participation, including self-selected turns). Building on the weaving metaphor first used by Tharp and Gallimore, Goldenberg describes how an instructional conversation develops:

> First, a skilled teacher weaves together the comments and contributions made by different students with the ideas and concepts she or he wishes to explore with them. Second, a teacher weaves students' prior knowledge and experiences with new knowledge and

experiences, thereby broadening the scope of their understanding while building upon understandings they already possess. Finally, during the course of conversation, a skilled teacher weaves together, in appropriate proportions and shadings, the 10 IC elements. While particular elements can be picked out and identified—just as threads of different color can be picked out and identified on a cloth—instruction and conversation are woven into a seamless whole: The conversation is instructional, and the instruction is conversational. (p. 319)

The reading lesson concludes with each of the learners recording an individual response in a writing journal. Learners are encouraged to reflect on and integrate ideas from the discussion groups in their personal responses. Writing entries are composed in the language of the learner's choice. The nature of the entries varies widely. Sometimes, they are brief, quick responses to a text and subsequent discussion, as in Figure 2.4, a parent's response to a reading titled "A Woman's Work Is Never Done."

At other times, written responses are prepared over longer periods and undergo the full process of planning, drafting, revising, and editing. In the next example, the parent wrote in response to a collection of readings from the local newspapers about increasing gang activity in the community. She composed first in Spanish and then in English. When she chose this particular piece to include in the project's annual publication of parents' writing, she spent additional time revising and editing it. It appears here in its final form:

> The gangs are groups of adolescents and adults. They use their clothing and signs to become identified. They have many names and many tattoos. When they join the gangs, they hit the new members they want to enter the gang. If they do not resist, they can stay. They are like a family because they can't exit.
>
> The gangs are in different places. The gangs are making trouble. I don't want my children in a gang. I saw on TV a program where adolescents spoke about wanting to leave the gang, but the others threatened them with killing someone from their family. Some of the gangs use drugs; also they steal and harm other people. I think that if my children belonged to a gang, I would feel bad, nervous, afraid, sad because I think that they can kill. I would look for help for myself so that I can speak with my children and help them to leave the gangs. I always ask God to take care of my children so that they will go a good way. Also, I speak with them about the gangs and about drugs and alcohol. (Intergenerational Literacy Project, 1996, p. 75)

Supporting adult literacy through writing lessons.   In addition to writing in response to reading, instruction is also planned to provide parents with opportunities to discuss and write about issues of importance in their personal and family lives. Two particular practices frame these writing opportunities: the development of personal narratives and the use of dialogue journals.

FIGURE 2.4   Unedited Journal Entry

Today is February   16, 2000
Do you agree? ~~Are you~~ ever done with
work at home?
How can your husband or older kids
help aut more for you?

1) No really I don't agree   ohly some times,
~~when it have   any~~ reseans for this.
    There are
For exampl my husband works at
night and when he comes back at
home he is so tiercl and he must
sleep.   tired
② Some times I think that I finish
every thing, ~~if~~ and I ~~sitdown.~~ ~~After~~
                        st
two minuts I remember Oh I have
and something to do.
Some times I finish by three o'clock
every thing is done but when
kids come back from school at
three   every thing is crazy.
③ Yes, if they want some ~~time~~
                                me
than can help~~me~~ a little bite ~~for~~ for
example : My husband cleans ~~leaving~~ room
My children take ✗ their
            the
clothing from floor, or
thei'n books.

41

Personal narratives.   As previously noted, the participants in the ILP are a diverse group, differing in age, gender, home country, language, culture, and family roles. Becoming a community of learners requires that participants have the opportunity to talk about who they are, where they have been, what they care about, and what they hope for. This talk routinely becomes the foundation for writing. As developing bilinguals, participants almost always choose to tell their stories first in their native language. They often prepare the first written draft in their native language as well, and later they rewrite their story in English. Their personal narratives typically undergo several revisions, and many are selected by parents for inclusion in the ILP's annual published anthology of the writings of parents and children or in the project's newspaper. Their stories tell of circumstances past and present, and they help us to "stay tuned" to their hopes and their dreams and to understand the complexity of their lives. Their narratives address a range of issues. A frequent topic is their journey to the United States, as in this example:

Immigrants Coming to the United States

Immigrants suffer a lot. They suffer from hunger, thirst, and the Coyotes [a Coyote is a person who brings people illegally] treat them very bad. They hit the poor immigrants, and the immigrants can't do anything because they are scared of being killed or being left in a place that they haven't been before. Some Coyotes take the extra money that the immigrants have for food and drinks. They rape the women and sometimes they become pregnant from the Coyotes. Most of the time the Coyotes hide the immigrants in the trunk of the car, and most of the time the immigrants suffocate because they don't get air inside the trunk.

My experience wasn't bad compared to other immigrants. When I was coming to the United States, I was lucky that the Coyote I was coming with wasn't bad like others. He took us to restaurants to eat good food. We ate bistec enseballado, and every day he brought us food. He spoke English and he was nice.

I was coming with my mother's aunt and her son and my mother's cousin. I was always with them. We slept in the same room. The Coyote took us to hotels. He left us in Los Angeles and in 1993 a Coyote who envied him killed him.

When I was in Los Angeles, it was March 25th, my birthday. I turned ten years old, but I wasn't yet with my mother. Two days later, I came to Boston with my mother's family by plane. Then when we got to my mother's house in Boston, I was scared of my father because I didn't know him. He came here when I was only three months old, and my mother came here when I was four years old. I didn't want to eat because I missed my grandma and I didn't like American food. But then I got to know my parents better and now I love them and I like American food.

Then in 1993 they celebrated my 15th birthday and on September 11 I got pregnant, and my parents didn't like it. My daughter was born in June

11, 1994. Now everyone is happy with my daughter and I am too. (Intergenerational Literacy Project, 1995, pp. 7-8)

Sometimes, parents write about experiences in their neighborhoods.

Walking across the Street

Last week when I came from school at eight o'clock, I walked across the street with my son. I saw four people. They had a knife—every one of them. Then they stabbed the front door of every household. When I saw them do that, I was between them. Then I stopped walking. My son was behind me; I was waiting for him. At the time, they stayed in the park. I don't know what happened after that. I was afraid about that. My son and I ran right to my house. (Intergenerational Literacy Project, 1995, p. 10)

Some parents tell of family relationships and how those relationships shaped them.

My Grandfather

My grandpa taught me many things. He taught me to farm, how to work the land, for example, sowing and cultivating seeds. He used to tell me that he wanted me to be a farmer, and he would tell me that I had to work hard to make a lot of money. I have experience because he gave me a lot of advice and I cherish everything he told me. He told me that he had a lot of land for us to cultivate. He also told us that he wanted us to be honorable men, and that we should respect our elders, always greeting them with great respect. (Intergenerational Literacy Project, 1996, p. 87)

Frequently, the conversation turns to issues that they would like their friends and neighbors to think about, and the resulting narratives are often didactic in tone.

Parents and Kids

Ever since I was twelve I knew what was good and what was not good. My parents were telling me all the time "Do this," or "Don't do that, that's not good." I think that it's good for parents to do this. Now I know they were right—parents always tell you to do good things, they never tell you to do bad things.

Every night when I go to work I see boys and girls who are twelve or thirteen years old out on the street. It's something that shouldn't be happening. It is time for young girls and boys to be sleeping; it's not time for them to be on the street, it's dangerous.

In this case, I think parents are responsible. I think the parents aren't telling the kids what to do and what not to do. If they do it from the time when the kids are six or eight years old, they will behave and obey when they are older. (Intergenerational Literacy Project 1994, p. 39)

The discourse that precedes the written narratives varies with the topic. Parents don't necessarily share the same experiences, opinions, and points of view. Sometimes the conversation is warm and supportive, and at other times it is confrontational and argumentative; almost always it is rich and interactive, and as such, it provides an important foundation for the writing that follows.

Dialogue journals.   Parents are paired with a teacher or tutor for dialogue journal writing. The journals are intended to serve as another context for conversation between learners and teachers. As such, learners are encouraged to write as much as they wish about any topic they choose. The teacher or tutor responds as a conversational partner (Bode, 1989; Kreeft-Peyton, 1986). Journals are exchanged throughout each week, and entries are completed both inside and outside class. Consistent with guidelines for the use of dialogue journal writing, entries are focused on topics of importance in the lives of the correspondents and on meaning rather than form (Bode, 1989; Kreeft-Peyton, 1986). The examples (unedited) presented here were composed by Carmen, a mother with two young daughters who attended the child care center, and John, a tutor. Carmen used the writing opportunity to discuss her own and her daughters' health, and John supported the dialogue by asking questions of Carmen and by expressing his admiration for all that she (and mothers in general) managed to do:

> Hi john,
>   This morning I not want to cam to the class but I cam for my daughters. Because they want to cam I not feel good this morning.

> I'm sorry you're not feeling well. Maybe you are getting a cold? Doctors say that February is the month with the most cases of the flu. I hope you are feeling better. How are your daughters?—John

> Hi john,
>   My daughters was seak they have cold all week, and this is the reason for I not came the class all week and today I left my daughters with my sister Mary she not can came the class because her boy only have one month and he have cold to I think she cane back went he have two month.

> I hope your daughters are better now. I know it is hard to take care of children. I worked up in day care yesterday, and after 3 hours, I was so tired. I don't know how mothers do it.

Supporting adult literacy through self-monitoring.   Learners keep individual portfolios in which they maintain a record of texts they have read and those they have written. Approximately once each month, they review these records and complete a self-assessment. In the example shown in Figure 2.5, Rosa evaluated the previous month's activities. Parents come to the ILP to achieve a number of different goals, and Rosa's assessment is representative of many others in its focus on multiple literacies:

FIGURE 2.5   Sample Completed Self-assessment

Rosa E Rodriguez   12 - 6 - 95

MONTHLY SELF-ASSESSMENT

1. Look back at your readings. Choose the article you liked best and tell why.

The First Americans
because learn about the first people of
american. Also I Can help to my children,
when they need know in the home work
about the first American.

2. What would you like to do better in reading?

I would like to do better pronounce

3. Look back at the pieces you have written. Choose your best one and tell why.

The thing I Like is the Jouneral
because I can't write what ever you
want to say

4. What would you like to do better in writing?

I would like More words.

7/92

the acquisition of content knowledge that will benefit her and her children; her focus on improving pronunciation of words while reading; her interest in choosing her own writing topics; and her interest in developing her language knowledge in order to improve her writing.

Supporting children's literacy.   The ILP is based on the premise that as parents improve their own literacy, the skills and knowledge they gain will promote literacy learning among their children. In addition, however, the evidence that a potential source of school difficulty lies in the "discontinuity between norms for appropriate communication at home and at school" (Florio-Ruane, 1987, p. 190) and the prevalence of this difficulty among children who are members of linguistic and cultural minorities underscore the importance of providing adults with direct and explicit instruction in literacy events and practices that will effectively prepare children for American schools. Thus, as part of the adult literacy classes, parents spend approximately half of their instructional time in lessons and conversations related to materials and strategies for supporting their children's literacy learning. In response to evidence that storybook reading is strongly correlated with children's success in early reading (Anderson, Hiebert, Scott, & Wilkinson, 1985; Bus, van Ijzendoorn, & Pellegrini, 1995; Clark, 1976; Durkin, 1966), primary emphasis is placed on shared storybook reading. Parents are introduced to books in English and other languages, and they discuss and practice effective storybook reading strategies. They are encouraged to check out books from the project's lending library, which each class visits weekly. Storybook-reading strategies are modeled and practiced in class, and parents are given time each day to discuss books they shared on the previous day with their children. In some classes, parents complete a reading response form describing their child's reaction to the storybook read. A sample completed form is presented in Figure 2.6.

In their own writing, parents often choose to comment on the importance of family storybook reading in their own lives and in those of their children. This narrative, which the parent selected for inclusion in the published anthology of family stories, conveys the enjoyment many parents derive from the storybook sharing:

> When I read books to my children, I feel good and happy because I try to understand and know something I didn't know before. I want to learn and help my children learn and understand what happened in the book. They like to listen to me read to them more and more. They ask me about things they don't understand. I try to explain things to them and talk with them. It's fun. I'm glad about that because to share a book with my daughters—to speak, to read—that makes us like friends, not just like a mother with her daughter. (Intergenerational Literacy Project, 1999, p. 2)

In addition to learning about children's books and storybook reading strategies, parents are also introduced to other practices that may assist them in supporting their children in school. For example, they discuss ways to assist their children with homework, the types of questions to ask their children about their school day, and the types

FIGURE 2.6   Sample Completed Shared Storybook Reading Response

READING RESPONSE

NAME: _Maritza Mendoro_

DATE: _12-6-95_

I read the book _IS your Mama a llama?_

with _My children Esmeralda and Erik_

This is what happened when I shared the book:

This book is wonderful for
the little children, because it has different
(quien?)
animals, and they asked
questions when I Read every
page, and they were so excited
because they waited until the
llama found her mother and
the other book is beatiful too
because they can imagine
                    imagine
How they can drow a Star. the name
of book is Drow me a Star

of questions to ask their children's teachers. Within two weeks of enrollment, parents are provided time and guidance in class to write a letter to their children's teacher. Rosa wrote to her son's teacher to convey her appreciation to the teacher for offering her son a satisfying experience and to let her know that she is studying English (Figure 2.7). The teacher, Mrs. Aikenhead, responded by affirming both the form of communication and Rosa's family literacy initiatives (Figure 2.8).

Parents are also taught how to document their children's uses of literacy at home by keeping a family literacy portfolio, and they discuss how to share the portfolio with their children's teachers during parent–teacher conferences. A full description of the Family Literacy Portfolio Project is provided in Chapter 4.

In addition to working through parents to affect the literacy lives of their children, the ILP also supports children's learning by providing high-quality child care to

FIGURE 2.7 Parent's Letter to a Teacher

October 4, 1995

Dear Mrs Aikenhead

I am writing to you to tell thank you because you is a good teacher my son Jon C. Rodriguez. He is very happy because you are wonderful teacher and treats good. I am reading in English because I am taking classes of English. In the Intergenerational Literacy project.

Sincerelly
Rosa Rodríguez
(mother)

FIGURE 2.8 Teacher's Response to Parent's Letter

Dear Ms. Rodriguez,   10/20/95

Thank you so much for your letter--
it made me feel great! I'm
glad Juan Carlos is happy in
school. He always has something
interesting to say, and I enjoy
having him in my class.
I think it's good for you and Juan C.
that you're taking classes at the
Intergenerational Literacy Project.

Sincerely,

maggie Aikenhead

children while their parents attend family literacy classes. During morning classes, child care is provided to preschool youngsters; during the evening classes, both preschool and schoolage children participate. The child care center is equipped with early childhood learning materials, including big books and companion little books, cloth and cardboard books for toddlers, writing materials and utensils, manipulative letters and story cards, and educational games. The program features a daily "story-time," accompanied by activities that encourage response to the stories and books children hear and read.

The program is organized by "centers" including a book corner, a writing corner, a creative dramatics corner, and a blocks and toys corner. Based on a weekly topic (e.g., bears, snow, rain) books are selected for reading aloud and for children to browse through. In addition, related activities are selected. For example, in conjunction with the topic "snow," children listen to Ezra Jack Keats's *A Snowy Day*, go outside to build a snowman (an activity that promotes extensive language use), bring snow inside to observe what would happen (as in the story), and make pictures and write stories about their own snowy adventures. Because participating children range in age from just a few months to four years, there is considerable flexibility and choice in how children participate and in how they are encouraged to respond. Consistent with research in the acquisition and development of literacy abilities, language development and language use are emphasized; tutors are trained to interact verbally with children within all contexts, whether they are reading and discussing a story or building with blocks. Rereadings of stories are core to the program, and children hear and are encouraged to retell the same story several times throughout a day or week, thus building a concept of story in preparation for their own reading and writing. The teacher–child ratio in the child care center is approximately three to one, permitting extensive language interaction and also allowing teachers and tutors to attend to the individual needs of the very young children. To help bridge home and school literacies, parents are provided a brief description of the book of the week and related events, along with suggestions for family literacy activities. An example is provided in Figure 2.9.

FIGURE 2.9   Suggestions for Family Literacy Activities Related to Child Care Center Book of the Week

The Intergenerational Literacy Project
CHILD CARE CENTER

BOOK OF THE WEEK: *THE LITTLE RED HEN,* by Paul Galdone

CONCEPTS: Animals, cooperative, sequence, cause and effect

CENTER ACTIVITIES: Act out stories, thumbprint animals, mouse made out of walnuts and felt, strawberries made out of walnuts, marshmallow dog, jello jigglers in shapes of animals, making a big book based on *Cat on the Mat*

OTHER BOOKS READ: *Ed Emberley's Big Orange Drawing Book*
Hatte and the Fox, by Mem Fox
The Little Mouse, the Red Ripe Strawberry and the Big Hungry Bear, by Don and Audrey Wood
Millions of Cats, by Wanda Gag
Rooster's Off to See the World, by Eric Carle
Cat on the Mat, by Brian Wildsmith

THINGS TO DO AT HOME

√ Read, reread, and talk about books. Encourage your child to retell the events the way they happened in the story.

√ Discuss the story *The Little Red Hen* and talk about what happened when the animals would not help the hen. Talk about cooperation. Ask your children to help you with some chores around the house. They can help you measure when you cook. They can set the table or part of it (such as the napkins or salt and pepper shakers).

Schoolage children who attend in the evening receive homework support, are given many opportunities to read to and with a teacher or tutor, and have opportunities to read and discuss chapter-length books in a project modeled after the book club program (McMahon, Raphael, Goatley, & Pardo, 1997).

Children's literacy development is also supported through collaboration with the classroom teachers of the schoolage children. Soon after enrollment, classroom teachers are notified that a family member of a child in their classroom has enrolled in the project. They are provided a description of the project, and they are encouraged to meet with the parents to discuss their experiences in the project and to invite the parent to share the family literacy portfolio. They are also provided a printed label to attach to the student's cumulative school record that identifies the child and the family as participants in the ILP (Figure 2.10).

Finally, during the last four years, teachers have been invited to participate in a series of professional development seminars led by the ILP director and focused on the development of effective home–school collaboration practices. The seminars are part of the Home–School Portfolio Project and are fully described in Chapter 4.

Monitoring Learning

Evaluation of the ILP has a dual focus. The first relates to individual learners and is directed toward assessing and helping learners to self-assess their own progress in literacy development. The second relates to the program itself and seeks to examine whether the practices in place are effective in meeting the needs of the families we serve.

In the case of assessment of individual learners, emphasis is on collecting evidence within the context of daily instruction. The contents of parents' portfolios are

FIGURE 2.10   Printed Label to Affix to Child's Cumulative School Record

The Intergenerational Literacy Project

A parent or other adult family member of this student has been enrolled in the Intergenerational Literacy Project during the 19__–19__ school year.
The means that s/he:

1. attends project classes providing instruction in adult literacy and strategies for enhancing family literacy;

2. regularly engages in and reports literacy interactions with children in the family;

3. maintains a portfolio for each child including samples and anecdotes concerning the child's uses of literacy at home.

You might wish to talk with parents about their involvement in the literacy program and invite them to share the child's home literacy portfolio with you.

fully described in Chapter 3; in brief, they include an intake interview, which provides general demographic information as well as an accounting of typical personal and family literacy practices reported by the parent on entry to the project; literacy logs; writing; running records; and self-assessments.

As well, since 1998, the project has participated in an evaluation sponsored by the Massachusetts Department of Education in which learners provide self-report data on entry to and exit from the program related to personal goals, English language proficiency, reading and writing habits, and interactions with their children's teachers. Also as part of this evaluation, classroom teachers of children whose parents participate in the project complete preparticipation and postparticipation questionnaires on the children's school performance. (Samples of these evaluation questionnaires are provided in Appendixes A and B).

To assess the effectiveness of the program in general, the daily attendance and program completion of every learner are monitored. As a matter of policy, when a participant is absent for two consecutive days, one of the teachers makes a phone call to inquire about the family's health and to make certain that all is well. When learners exit the program, an exit interview is conducted, during which learners are asked to evaluate the effectiveness of the program in meeting their needs and to share their reasons for leaving.

Summary

The ILP began in 1989 with three purposes: to improve the English literacy of parents, to support the literacy development and academic success of their children, and to conduct research on the effectiveness of an intergenerational approach to literacy learning. It was implemented as part of a school–university comprehensive school reform effort. In this chapter, a detailed description was provided of the educational principles on which the project was founded and of the instructional activities and events that are offered to adults and their children. The next chapter focuses on evidence of project effectiveness.

NOTES

1. Since its beginning, the Intergenerational Literacy Project has received funding from many public and private agencies, including the United States Department of Education, Early Childhood Institute, FIRST Program, the Massachusetts Department of Education, the Annenberg Foundation, the Burden Foundation, the Lynch Foundation, the Ratchevsky Foundation, Xerox Corporation, Anna B. Stearns Foundation, the Clipper Ship Foundation, the Keel Foundation, the Barbara Bush Foundation, A Different September Foundation, Anna B. Stearns Charitable Foundation, the Deluxe Check Corporation, New England Telephone Corporation, Voyager III Parent Grant, Ramlose Foundation, Henry Meyer Jr., and Harold Whitworth Pierce.

3 Is It Working?
Reviewing the Evidence

One day Ernesto came and told me that he doesn't read to his son and we talked about his reasons and I made some suggestions. The next day, he bounded into class, early and truly excited. He had brought a book he and his son picked out together at the library. He reported that they took it home and read it. They had so much fun, the son asked to hear it again. Ernesto, beaming, said, "That never happened before. Never, never! And we had so much fun—I changed my voice like, 'Daddy, are we lost?' " Ernesto and his son read the book three times. He modeled some pages for the class, retelling the book's story and his own. He also sent me a mailbox letter about the event, ending with "Thank you-you-you."

—As told by Heidi, an ILP teacher

Recently, I stopped by Leonsa's house because she missed a few days of class. When I got there, she was delighted to see me and told me that the reason she hadn't been to class was that the electricity had been turned off and a lot of her time has been devoted to trying to get it back on. Leonsa's apartment is a floor-through on the top floor of a triple decker. She has no telephone, few toys for José and Pedro and only four or five books—all of them shredded, scribbled-on Golden Books. There's a couch in the kitchen, two chairs in the living room and two beds and a crib in a tiny bedroom. It would be a pretty depressing place, except for its most distinctive feature: the wall decorations. In both the living room and the bedroom, Leonsa has carefully tacked up every ILP certificate she, José, and Pedro have received (a total of ten).

—As told by Barbara, an ILP teacher

These anecdotes are only two of many that document in different ways the sense of accomplishment felt by many—we believe most—of the families who participate in the ILP. We know, because parents and children tell us, that participating in the ILP has opened new doors for them. But we also know because they show us—in the regularity with which they attend class, in the length of time that they choose to participate, in the stories that they read and write, and in the ways that they interact with and support their children in school.

The ILP's evaluation program is designed to capture both types of evidence—what parents tell us and what they show us. Through evaluation, we seek to learn whom we serve, why they come, why they stay, and why they leave. We also hope to determine whether participation in the program has positive outcomes, educational and otherwise, for the particular parents and children who attend. As with all components of the ILP, the assessment design is grounded in certain theoretical assumptions.

Theoretical Assumptions

In recent years, particular forms of school assessment have often been referred to as "high stakes," meaning that for many students in particular and for school institutions in general, the results have serious, even harmful, consequences. In the case of schoolage children, consequences of low test performance often include labeling, retention, and failure to graduate. For adults outside a particular institutional structure, consequences are somewhat less measurable but may include diminished access to particular employment opportunities, as well as societal labeling and stigmatization. For "special" programs such as the ILP, which exist year to year on "soft" money, the stakes are institutional and often funding related: low test scores may mean diminished financial support, thus putting the entire program at risk. As a result, choosing an accurate and appropriate evaluation program is of critical importance, both individually and programmatically. But how do we measure the construct we call "family literacy"? How do we account for what adults and children are taking from their experiences in such programs? How do we measure the meaning of such programs in their lives?

In 1989, Taylor and Strickland commented on the lack of congruence between the ways families use literacy to negotiate their daily activities and the ways in which literacy is traditionally assessed in schools:

> Solitary and shared, deliberate and momentary, social–interactional, news-related, and recreational, literacy is a complex, multi-dimensional phenomenon that can be described and appraised. In family settings literacy can be teased apart and examined but we can never account for it with numbers and tests. (p. 263)

A few years later, reflecting on the state of knowledge in the field of family literacy, Purcell-Gates (1993) also addressed the particular obstacles that confront family literacy investigators:

> Research into ways in which families embrace literacy-related activities suffers from the same constraints faced by the U.S. Census: How does one find out in valid and reliable ways what *really* goes on in homes? (p. 671)

And later, writing about her decade of work in a Latino community in California, Delgado-Gaitan (1996), too, commented on the challenge of appropriately representing the effects of family-based intervention programs:

During the years I have spent as a researcher in Carpinteria, I have made many public presentations where people have asked me how much the Latino children in Carpinteria improved their grades as a result of their parents' involvement in their children's education. People have felt unsatisfied when I responded with a lengthy and involved answer which, in essence, meant that learning is a lifelong process and that the COPLA [Comite de Padres Latinos] parents have learned a great deal from each other, but it has been through their years together. A change of grade on student report cards and accelerated test scores alone represent narrow perspectives of parent involvement in education. Children's academic accomplishments are born of parents' commitment to support them in their education. Put differently, parents can be quite actively involved in a child's school, at a time of crisis, the test and grade outcome remain unaffected. Even though parents may be actively involved in their children's education, children's grades may plummet at different times during their schooling as a result of complicated circumstances. Yet children have a stronger possibility to socially and academically recover as a result of their family's support. A child may become empowered over time as a result of the parents' consistent intervention and support even though the outcomes are not immediately evident as was the case with Carpinteria families. (pp. 11–12)

The complexity of assessing the effects of family literacy intervention programs is underscored further by Serpell (1997):

As I understand it, for a developing individual, the process of becoming literate includes two complementary facets: induction into membership of a community of practice . . . and subjective appropriation of a cultural meaning-system. . . . Full membership of a community implies entitlement to ownership of its cultural resources . . . which in the case of a literate community, includes both the technology of writing and the meaning-system that informs literate practices. Appropriation of cultural practice involves not only the adoption of resources that were created by earlier generations such as the language; the script; and the law, religion, and science embodied in the corpus of the culture's accumulated wisdom. It also involves reflective application of these preexisting resources to the individual's own personal experience, and the gradual crafting of a personal perspective on the world, utilizing (and to some extent accepting domination by) the constraints of that culture. (p. 588)

Comments such as these, as well as work in assessment in general, caused us to think long and hard about how to accurately and appropriately represent what parents and children know and do in relation to literacy and the ways the ILP influences their literate actions. From the start, we intended assessment to inform how we shaped the program generally and how we planned instruction specifically. As noted in Chapter 2, we were influenced in our assessment design by the work by Archbald and Newmann (1988), who argued that assessment should be conducted in authentic contexts, exemplified by three essential traits: they engage students in tasks that approximate those that experts perform, they require students to join the pieces of a project into an integrated whole, and they have utility beyond evaluation. In its final iteration, our stance toward assessment is effectively articulated in a recent position paper of the

International Reading Association (1999): "Assessment is the purposeful collection of data to inform actions. From the viewpoint of educators, the primary purpose of assessment is to help students by providing information about how instruction can be improved" (p. 258).

Assessment Measures We Use

Consistent with a view of literacy as complex, multidimensional, and socially important and a perspective that trustworthy literacy assessment must be grounded within contexts that are similarly complex, multidimensional, and socially important, we chose to gather evidence of participants' literacy practices within contexts and activities that are consistent with the literacy actions they take at home and at school. Specifically, parents keep individual portfolios in which they store several types of artifacts that document their literacy development. One is an intake interview (Appendix A), which provides general demographic information as well as a report of their reasons for enrolling in the program, an account of typical personal and family literacy practices reported by the parent on entry to the project, and a report of their impressions of their children's school performance. This information is useful to us and to the learners when we look back over time and assess the ways in which their literacy practices have changed. Another is the daily literacy log (described in Chapter 2), in which learners report their uses of reading and writing alone and with their children.

Portfolios also hold learners' daily writing, which includes both reading response pieces and original narrative and nonnarrative writing. In the case of parents who are learning to decode print, the portfolio includes a record of their oral reading fluency, which is documented at the beginning and end of the project year by using running records (Clay, 1985). On their exit from the program, learners complete an exit interview (Appendix B) that asks many of the same questions asked during the intake interview. It includes a report of their progress toward their personal goals, their uses of reading and writing alone and with their children during a typical day and week, and their impressions of their children's school performance. This also becomes part of their portfolio.

To assess the effectiveness of the program in general, we monitor the daily attendance and program completion of every learner. When a learner leaves the program, an exit interview is conducted, during which learners are asked to evaluate the effectiveness of the program in meeting their needs and to share their reasons for leaving. Figure 3.1 presents a summary of the evaluation measures we use to monitor project effectiveness.

What Have We Learned?

In this section, the findings are presented in three sections. First, I present data that describe the families who participated in the ILP's first ten years; next, I present data related to programmatic outcomes, including attention, retention, and achievement data; finally, I present three case studies to exemplify the ways individuals develop and use literacy during their participation in the ILP.

Who Does the Intergenerational Literacy Project Serve?

During the first ten years of the project, 1,330 adults and 3,535 children participated in the ILP. As Table 3.1 indicates, most of the adults who participated were mothers, but many other caregivers also enrolled, including fathers, grandparents, aunts, uncles, and older siblings. The families were mostly new immigrants, with nearly 60 percent having resided in the United States for five or fewer years and nearly 20 percent for less than one year. They represented 46 different countries of origin (Table 3.2) and spoke 23 different first languages (Table 3.3). Nearly three-quarters of the adults described themselves on entry as speaking little or no English.

On average, adult participants had completed eight years of schooling in their own countries. Most (70 percent) reported that they were able to read in their first language, and 20 percent reported that they were able to read in English. Their self-reports indicate that, outside of reading and writing personal letters, which most participants reported doing frequently to stay in contact with family members in their home countries, they engage in personal reading and writing primarily for notational purposes, reading mail, and writing shopping lists. In addition, review of intake data indicated that about half of the participants engaged in family storybook reading or storytelling at least occasionally on entry. Few, however, reported that they visited the library (11 percent) or bought books (8 percent). Almost 40 percent reported that they were employed outside the home either full-time or part-time.

Although parents came to the ILP because they were committed to their children's learning, it is also clear that they were motivated to participate by very explicit

TABLE 3.1 Family Roles of Intergenerational Literacy Project Participants

	Year 1	Year 2	Year 3	Year 4	Year 5	Year 6	Year 7	Year 8	Year 9	Year 10	Total
Number of families enrolled	74	130	163	96	132	181	189	212	161	198	1,536
Mothers	54	80	112	65	90	107	134	142	103	127	1,014
Fathers	8	35	29	15	24	26	23	34	22	21	237
Grandmothers	6	9	11	8	7	18	16	11	10	8	104
Grandfathers	0	0	1	1	2	9	7	4	6	3	33
Aunts	4	3	3	4	3	3	2	6	8	19	55
Uncles	2	2	4	1	6	11	4	13	7	11	61
Siblings	0	0	1	1	0	2	2	1	3	2	12
Others	0	1	2	1	0	5	1	1	2	7	20

FIGURE 3.1   Assessment Measures

Purpose of the Measure	Assessment Measure	Project Participant
To describe the population served	Intake Interview	Parents
To assess writing proficiency	Writing Samples	Parents
To assess reading proficiency	Running Records	Parents
To assess family literacy practices	Literacy Log	Parent
	Questionnaire/ Interview	Parent
To assess personal literacy practices	Questionnaire/ Interview	Parent
To assess influence of project on child's school success	Questionnaire/ Interview	Parent
		Child's Teacher
To assess learners' interest and motivation in project activities	Attendance	Parent
	Questionnaire/ Interview	Parent

personal goals. For these immigrant families, the most frequently stated personal goal was to "read, write, and speak English."

What Are the Programmatic and Learning Outcomes?

Earlier reports of project effectiveness indicated that attendance and retention rates in the ILP exceeded those of traditional adult education programs (Paratore, 1993, 1994), that parents made gains in oral reading fluency at a rate that exceeded gains made by adults in traditional adult literacy programs (Paratore, 1993, 1994), and that parents increased the frequency with which they engaged their children in shared literacy events (Paratore, 1993, 1994). Further, in-depth case studies of the home and

Types of Data Included	Data Collection Procedures
Participant characteristics	Individually administered within two weeks of enrollment
Drafts and final copies of in-class writing assignments	Narratives and essays written during the context of daily instruction are filed in the learners' portfolios; on entry and exit, learners write in a directed prompt
Oral reading fluency and comprehension	Individually administered to adults identified as new or beginning readers
Self-report of literacy events shared with child	Completed by each parent daily as part of literacy class routines
Self-report of literacy events shared with child during a typical week	Completed individually or with a group on entry and exit from the project
Self-report of literacy events engaged in to meet personal goals during a typical week	Completed individually or with a group on entry and exit from the project
Attitude, academic performance, attendance, parent–teacher contact	Completed individually or with a group on entry and exit from the project
	Questionnaire mailed to teacher within two weeks of family's enrollment and on family's exit from the project
Attendance in daily classes	Recorded by adult literacy teacher daily
Reasons for enrolling, reasons for staying, reasons for leaving	Completed individually or with a group on entry and exit from the project

school literacy experiences of schoolage children whose parents participated in the project indicated that most of the children studied experienced either high or average levels of success in school (Paratore, Melzi, & Krol-Sinclair, 1999). These successful learners shared many important family and school characteristics: frequent and consistent literacy interactions with a parent, consistent monitoring of school performance by a parent, systematic and effective literacy instruction in school, excellent attitudes and behavior toward school and learning, and high school attendance. The only factor that distinguished the highly successful learners from the moderately successful learners was their length of time in the United States, with children who were identified as newcomers achieving slightly below those who had been in the country for three or more years. Unlike the children who experienced school success, those who struggled

TABLE 3.2 Countries of Origin of Families in the Intergenerational Literacy Project

	Year 1	Year 2	Year 3	Year 4	Year 5	Year 6	Year 7	Year 8	Year 9	Year 10	Total
Argentina	0	0	0	0	0	0	0	1	0	0	1
Armenia	4	0	0	0	0	0	0	0	0	1	5
Bolivia	1	1	2	1	1	0	0	0	0	0	6
Bosnia	0	0	0	0	0	0	0	6	10	12	28
Brazil	0	0	0	0	0	1	5	6	2	1	15
Cambodia	3	23	20	8	6	1	1	0	0	3	65
Cape Verde	1	1	0	1	0	3	2	2	0	1	11
Chile	0	0	1	0	0	0	0	1	0	0	2
China	0	1	0	0	0	0	0	0	1	1	3
Colombia	2	4	4	2	3	6	9	14	7	12	63
Costa Rica	2	3	9	3	4	1	3	0	2	3	30
Croatia	0	0	0	0	0	0	0	0	0	1	1
Cuba	1	0	0	0	0	0	0	0	0	0	1
Curaçao	0	0	1	0	0	0	0	0	0	0	1
Dominican Republic	2	9	9	5	5	18	17	13	8	6	92
Egypt	0	0	1	0	0	0	0	0	0	1	2
El Salvador	17	22	22	19	38	45	28	45	38	60	334
Eritrea	0	0	0	0	0	0	0	0	0	1	1
Ethiopia	0	0	0	0	0	0	3	0	0	0	3
Guatemala	8	8	15	10	14	38	41	39	34	25	232
Haiti	1	1	1	0	0	1	0	2	6	2	14
Honduras	7	2	10	15	25	32	16	35	19	18	179
Hong Kong	0	0	0	0	0	0	2	3	2	0	7
Jamaica	1	0	0	0	0	0	0	0	0	0	1
Japan	0	0	0	0	0	0	0	1	0	1	2
Jordan	0	0	0	0	0	0	0	0	0	1	1
Laos	0	1	0	0	0	0	0	0	0	0	1
Mexico	2	3	2	3	3	2	6	6	4	8	39
Moldavia	0	0	0	0	0	0	1	0	0	0	1
Morocco	0	0	0	0	0	1	0	0	2	6	9
Nicaragua	1	1	0	0	2	2	0	0	0	0	6
Palestine	0	0	0	0	0	0	0	0	0	2	2
Panama	0	0	0	0	0	0	0	1	1	0	2
Peru	2	1	2	3	0	1	6	2	0	4	21
Philippines	0	0	0	0	0	1	0	0	0	0	1
Poland	0	1	0	0	0	0	1	3	0	1	6
Portugal	1	0	0	0	0	0	0	0	0	0	1
Puerto Rico	8	14	30	18	22	24	41	21	17	9	204
Russia	0	0	0	0	0	0	0	1	0	0	1
Saudi Arabia	0	0	0	0	0	0	0	0	0	1	1
Serbia	0	0	0	0	0	0	0	0	1	0	1
Somalia	0	0	0	0	0	0	0	4	4	15	23
Trinidad	1	0	0	0	0	1	0	0	0	0	2

	Year 1	Year 2	Year 3	Year 4	Year 5	Year 6	Year 7	Year 8	Year 9	Year 10	Total
United States	7	5	1	1	2	0	0	1	1	0	18
Venezuela	1	1	0	0	0	2	3	1	1	0	9
Vietnam	1	28	33	7	7	1	4	4	1	2	88

TABLE 3.3 First Languages Spoken by Families in the Intergenerational Literacy Project

	Year 1	Year 2	Year 3	Year 4	Year 5	Year 6	Year 7	Year 8	Year 9	Year 10	Total
Arabic	0	0	1	0	0	1	0	0	2	10	14
Armenian	4	0	0	0	0	0	0	0	0	1	5
Bosnian	0	0	0	0	0	0	0	5	8	12	25
Cape Verdean Creole	0	0	0	1	0	3	2	2	0	1	9
Chinese	0	1	1	0	0	0	2	3	2	1	10
Dutch	0	0	1	0	0	1	0	0	0	0	2
English	10	5	1	1	2	0	0	0	1	0	20
French	0	0	1	0	0	0	0	0	0	0	1
Hmong	0	1	0	0	0	0	0	0	0	0	1
Japanese	0	0	0	0	0	0	0	1	0	1	2
Khmer	3	20	22	12	6	1	1	0	1	3	69
Kreyol (Haitian Creole)	1	1	0	0	0	1	0	2	6	2	13
Mharic	0	0	0	0	0	0	3	0	0	0	3
Moldavian	0	0	0	0	0	0	1	0	0	0	1
Polish	0	1	0	0	0	0	1	3	0	1	6
Portuguese	2	1	0	0	0	1	5	6	2	1	18
Russian	0	0	0	0	0	0	0	1	0	0	1
Serbo-Croatian	0	0	0	0	0	0	0	1	3	1	5
Somali	0	0	0	0	0	0	0	4	4	15	23
Spanish	53	69	105	79	117	171	170	180	131	146	1,221
Tagalog	0	0	0	0	0	1	0	0	0	0	1
Tigrean	0	0	0	0	0	0	0	0	0	1	1
Vietnamese	1	31	31	3	7	1	4	4	1	2	85

had little in common. Three had frequent literacy interactions with a parent; one only occasionally shared literacy with a family member. Three had a parent who monitored homework daily; one did not. Two had systematic and effective literacy instruction in school; two did not. Two experienced school transience; the others did not. Two had difficult family circumstances including divorce and substance abuse; two did not. One was believed to have a learning disability. The picture that emerged was not one in which school failure could be explained by what parents did or did not do but rather one in which school failure is understood as the consequence of an array of difficult circumstances that challenge some children both in and out of school.

Since the publication of these studies, additional data have been collected. In the section that follows, new evidence of the outcomes related to participation in the ILP is presented.

Attendance and retention.   As traditional measures of program quality in adult education, we have continued to examine attendance and retention data as measures of learners' motivation and interest in learning. Following the often heard dictum in adult education that "adults vote with their feet," we have held to the premise that in programs that effectively address the needs of adult participants, attendance and retention rates will be high. Throughout the first ten years of the project, attendance and retention data have been kept on every learner who has enrolled and remained in the project for at least two weeks. The results suggest a remarkably stable attendance rate, averaging 72 percent over the ten-year period and varying little, from a low of 68 percent (in 1993–94) to a high of 76 percent (in 1998–99). This rate compares very favorably against an average attendance rate of approximately 50 percent in adult education programs nationally (Sticht, 1988–89).

The average retention rate across the ten-year period was 74 percent.[1] This rate distinguishes the ILP as outperforming both traditional adult education and other family literacy programs when retention is used as a criterion measure. Sticht (1988–89) reported 50 percent as the average retention rate for traditional adult education programs; Tao, Swartz, St. Pierre, and Tarr (1997) reported 64 percent as the average rate of retention in a study of 458 family literacy programs funded by the federal Even Start legislation. Parents report three primary reasons for leaving the program prior to the end of an instructional cycle: to begin a new job or a new job schedule; to resolve family difficulties, often related to health and housing; or to pursue a graduate equivalency degree or other course work. Mothers also interrupt their period of study because of pregnancy, but many of these women re-enroll at a later date.

High attendance and retention rates are encouraging indicators. They tell us that parents who participate in the ILP are committed to learning. They also tell us that program activities are such that parents consider attendance worthy of their time and effort. But they tell us little about whether parents are advancing toward the literacy goals they have set for themselves and their children. To examine changes in literacy knowledge, we conducted an analysis of data collected during the 1997–98 project year from a random selection of 42 parents. We relied on three primary data sources. The first was a questionnaire, completed by parents at the beginning and end of the project year (Appendixes A and B). On the questionnaire, which parents chose to complete either orally or in writing, participants rated their progress in reading and writing and reported on their uses of reading and writing during a typical week alone and with their children. They also recorded their impressions of their children's performance in school. Writing samples provided a second source of data. These were collected from adults at the beginning and end of the project year. Elementary classroom teachers provided a third source of data; they completed questionnaires about schoolage children's school performance during the project year.

Changes in parents' literacy. As a group, parents in the sample perceived themselves as having made steady progress toward their reading and writing goals, with 98 percent reporting that they had made progress in reading and 90 percent reporting that they had made progress in writing. They were asked to give explicit examples of how their reading or writing had changed. In reading, learners said that they understood more of what they read, increased their ability to read different books, read magazines and newspapers more often, were able to read more difficult words, and were better able and more confident when reading with their children. When asked, they provided specific titles of books and magazines that they read now and were unable to read previously. In writing, learners noted increased ability in writing notes and letters, checks and bills, work-related writing, and their homework.

Another indication of advancement in literacy is the extent to which participants increased the types and frequency of literacy uses in the context of their daily lives. Figure 3.2 presents changes in parents' reported uses of literacy alone and with their children. Preinstructional and postinstructional reports showed small but consistent

FIGURE 3.2 Weekly Family Literacy Practices

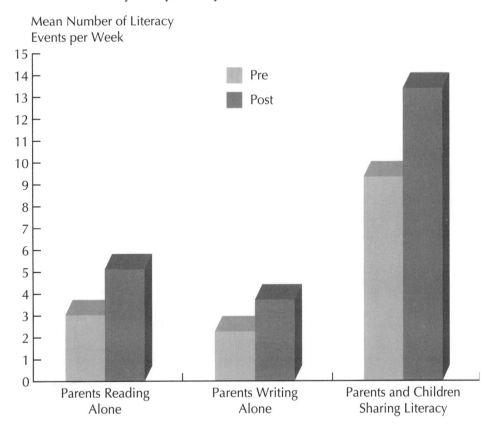

increases in both their personal uses of reading and writing and in parent–child literacy interactions.

There were also several areas of change noted in the ways parents and children shared literacy on a daily basis (Figure 3.3). Parents reported notable increases in storytelling and storybook reading and smaller increases in homework monitoring and homework support. Weekly changes (Figure 3.4) were even more substantial, with better than 80 percent of all parents reporting at least weekly engagement in storybook reading and storytelling, literacy events that received substantial attention in the parents' literacy classes.

We also measured changes in parents' literacy by analyzing writing samples. With an average of 28 weeks of instruction between samples, writing performance changed from a mean score of 5.3 on preinstruction samples to a mean score of 7.1 on postinstruction samples. According to the writing evaluation rubric used (Appendix C), these scores indicate that, on average, learners advanced from the level of "developing" writer to the level of "adequate writer" during the period of study.

Changes in children's literacy.   A total of 23 teachers, representing 20 primary grade and 3 intermediate grade students, returned questionnaires mailed to them at

FIGURE 3.3   Types of Daily Parent–Child Literacy Interactions

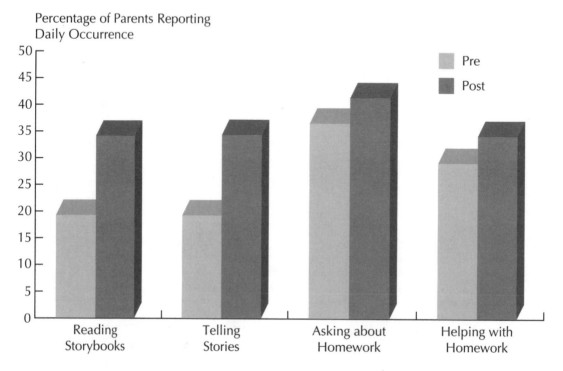

Percentage of Parents Reporting
Daily Occurrence

FIGURE 3.4   Types of Weekly Parent–Child Literacy Interactions

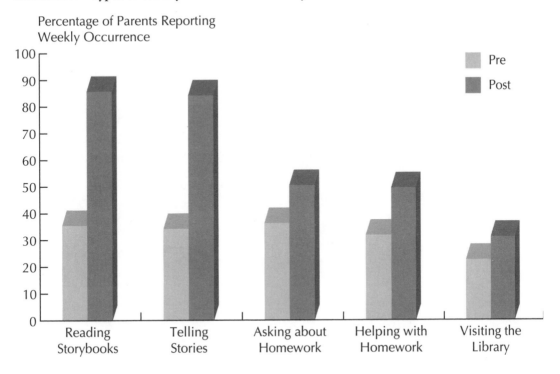

the beginning and end of the project year. As shown in Figure 3.5, at the beginning of the project year, teachers rated students as having positive attitudes toward school and learning, and their ratings remained unchanged at the end of the year. In rating academic performance, teachers' initial evaluations indicated that, on average, children performed at about the level of the average child—a rating of 3.8 on a 5-point scale. In their final evaluations, the mean rating increased slightly to 4.2, placing the children slightly above average in academic achievement. At the end of the year, teachers were also asked to rate the students' performance in literacy specifically, both in relation to native language and English reading. In native language reading, the mean rating placed students, as a group, above grade level; in English reading, the mean rating placed children, as a group, slightly below grade level (Figure 3.6).

Parents were also asked to provide their impressions of their children's academic performance at the beginning and end of their enrollment in the project, and their impressions were highly consistent with those of the classroom teachers. On average, parents perceived that their children began and ended the school year with good attitudes toward school and learning. They also judged their children as having good rates

FIGURE 3.5   Teachers' Report of Children's School Achievement

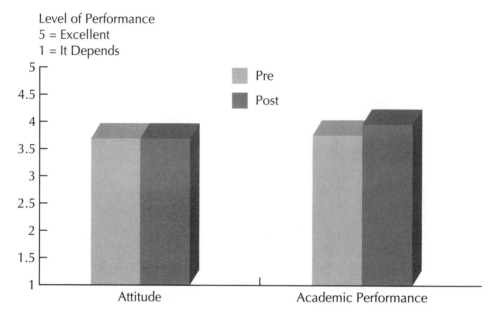

FIGURE 3.6   Teachers' Report of Children's End-of-year Reading Achievement

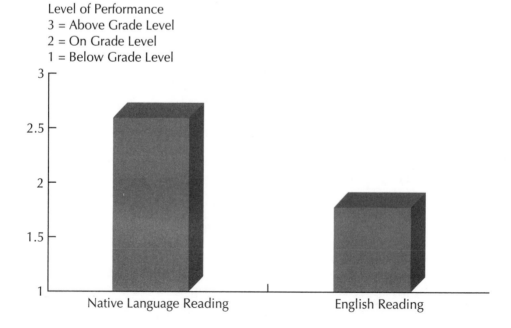

FIGURE 3.7   Parents' Report of Children's School Achievement

Level of Performance
5 = Excellent
1 = Don't know

of performance at both the beginning and end of the year, although their evaluations were slightly higher at the end of the school year (Figure 3.7).

Portraits of Individual Learners

The preceding evidence may be helpful in understanding the general effects of the ILP on the families it serves. But often, group results obscure the meaning of projects such as the ILP in the lives of the families who participate. To better understand what families take from their ILP experiences, I have chosen to tell the stories of a few. I have selected these particular cases not because they stand out from any other but rather because they do not, and they therefore provide a glimpse into the experiences of many of the families we serve.

Maritza.   Maritza first enrolled in the ILP in June 1990. At that time she had resided in the United States for two and a half years; she had two children, a six-year-old boy and a five-month-old girl, and she was pregnant with her third child. She learned about the ILP from a friend, and she came so that she could learn to read, write, and speak in English. Maritza had completed eight years of schooling in El Salvador. During her intake interview, she described herself as having no proficiency in English. She said that at home, she sometimes read newspapers in Spanish and she also read her mail. She wrote letters to her mother in El Salvador, and she wrote shopping lists.

She reported that she had never visited the library but that she shared stories with her son, José, who was then a first grader, once or twice a week. She said that she checked her son's homework a few times each week and helped with homework "whenever—every day if necessary." She said she did not write notes or messages to her son and, when asked if she wrote to or met with his teacher, she responded, "Not often." She said she knew about José's school performance from his teacher's reports and from observing him at home, and she described him as a "good" reader but "better with math."

At the end of her first 15-week cycle of study, Maritza left the ILP to give birth to her third child. She returned more than three years later in February 1994 and stayed until May 1996. At the time of her re-enrollment, José was ten years old and in the sixth grade; her daughter, Esmeralda, was four years old and attended the school district's early childhood program; and her son Erik was three years old and attended the ILP child care. On returning, she redefined her goals as "more speaking and writing in English" and "so I can help my kids." She described her English proficiency as "better than minimal" but not moderate. Her responses to interview questions indicated that her children influenced the ways she used literacy at home. For example, when asked what she read at home, she said that she shared stories with her children daily and specifically reported reading *Little Red Riding Hood* in Spanish and *Beauty and the Beast* "with my daughter in English." She said she asked her children about their homework every day and helped when she could but that the "homework is all in English." She said that she "never" met with her children's teachers but that she read information sent home from school. When the information proved difficult, she asked her son for help. He often translated words into Spanish for her, and he also "looked over" her writing.

Both on entry and throughout her participation in the project, when Maritza was asked to set goals, to self-assess her progress, and to monitor the effectiveness of the classes, she emphasized her desire to improve her oral and written English proficiency. The following unedited response was commonplace:

> I would like to write better in English because is very important when I have to fill out applications or when I has to fill out bills too or send a letter for somebody who does not understand Spanish. (11-30-95)

We focused assessment largely on evidence of change in writing. During her first cycle of participation in 1990, Maritza made no attempt to write in English. All portfolio writing samples were in Spanish. When she rejoined the program in 1994, during the initial months, she continued to compose in Spanish. Her first written entry in English was dated June 1994 and is reproduced in unedited form:

> I go to visit to my father and new yersey for one week with my family and new yersey have sister brother.

Several months later (February 1995), her unedited writing showed signs of significant growth:

> The most important person in my life is my mother because she lived old the time at home. She taught and gave advice about when I was growing up. Also she helped with my homework. I remember her everyday because she is a good person. I think my father too but he all the time work and do not haved time.

Maritza's English writing continued to improve, and by February 1996 she had extended the length, linguistic complexity, and grammatical accuracy of her writing:

> When I was a child I lived in El Salvador. I remember when I was four years old. My earliest memory is when I played with my sister's doll. I remember when I made dresses for my doll. When my sister saw what I made she told me please make some for my doll because she didn't like to try to make things for her doll. Another thing is that I remember when I started first grade I liked to play jacks. After we finished a class we liked to play with the other girls. When I arrived at my home, my mother waited for us because we took more time than normal and she was angry with us and she gave us both punishment because we both disobeyed her.

Beyond growth in writing, literacy logs also provide evidence of Maritza's investment and dedication to her children's literacy learning. From the start, her daily entries focused on reading, writing, and speaking with her children. As the following collection of entries shows, in the beginning, she wrote briefly, but as her English proficiency improved, her entries became more elaborate:

> Today I help to my children with his homework. I read the book of the wheel and the bus. (12-6-94)
>
> Yesterday I asked my little children about how was their day and they answered we're doing well. My daughter she told me that the teacher gave her a sticker because she paid attention when the teacher told the children to pay attention at the class. (10-19-95)
>
> Yesterday I shared with my little children some story. The name of the book is the golden hen. This story speak about one little girl. She was good with any people. One day she saw a hen and found a hen was hurt and she took it home and help the hen. After the hen is much better she made an egg gold. Before she are poor. Now she are rich because every day she have a golden egg. (11-30-95)
>
> Yesterday I went to the store with my children and I looked for some books. My old son bought a book. The name of the book is Goose Bumps Number Two. This book talks about a goose and what a child imagines about them and my son likes a lot. He wants to draw too. (2-22-96)

Along with members of her class, at the start of the school year, Maritza composed letters to each of her children's teachers to let them know her interest and concern about her children's schooling. She planned her letters carefully, considering the needs of each youngster and writing accordingly:

Dear Mr. Obashown,

I send this letter about my son José Flores because I would like to know how he is doing in class because sometimes I am worried about his behavior at school. I would like to help him more in math because I know that he needs help. Please tell me how I can help him.

Sincerely,
Maritza M. Flores

Dear Mrs. Ferrante,

I write to you because I want to know about Erik Flores's behavior. Sometimes at home he becomes lazy and I would like to know if he's the same in your class. Please let me know anything that you are concerned with. Thank you very much for taking the time to read this letter. You can always send me a note or give a call at 887-0000.

Sincerely,
Maritza M. Flores

Dear Mrs. Cordero,

I am writing to thank you for all the things you are doing with my daughter. I know she is learning a lot. She tells me about you many times about the stickers that you give her if she does something good and I know she loves to go to school. Thank you very much for the time you dedicate to Esmeralda.

Sincerely,
Her mother
Maritza M. Flores

In school, two of Maritza's children have done well. Erik and Esmeralda, now fourth-graders, both achieved above-average performances on the state-mandated standardized reading achievement test given at the end of third grade. Her older son, José, attends the community vocational education school.

Maritza left the project in May 1996. She presently works as a patient care assistant in a nursing home, a position for which she was required to pass a two-part test comprising a written and a practical section (e.g., demonstrate appropriate handwashing or appropriate ways to lift a patient). The test is given in English only. She continues to stop into the project on occasion to let us know how she is doing and sometimes even to sit in on classes for a few weeks, a kind of "refresher" in family literacy.

Hung Mei.   Hung Mei enrolled in the ILP in October 1995. At the time of enrollment, she had resided in the United States for one year and in Chelsea for just six months. Her only child was an eight-month-old girl, Winger Ma. Hung Mei had attended school in her own country, Hong Kong, for nine years. She learned about the

ILP from a friend. She reported that at home she read newspapers and letters in Chinese and that she wrote letters and shopping lists in Chinese. She described her oral proficiency in English as moderate and enrolled in the project because she hoped to learn to speak, write, and read in English. She said that she visited the library once a week and shared stories with her child once a week. She remained in the ILP for three years. During her period of enrollment, she took a two-month leave of absence to give birth to her second child, Jeffrey, born in November 1996.

As is the case with most of the parents who participate in the ILP, Hung Mei's interest in her children and her children's education was evident from the very start of her enrollment. During the first week, her literacy log included the following (unedited) entries:

10-2   I all afternoon use the dictionary find the words and teach my kids.

10-3   I with my baby and husband to east Boston take ferry to Boston Aquarium watch fish vere nice

10-4   I read christmas book with my baby and paly toy

10-5   I borrowed Caps, Hats, Socks and Mittens stories in the library for my baby. I took it home enjoy it. My baby listened to the tape she liked it very much

10-9   I went with my baby and my husband to shopp. I buy the new dress for my baby. She watched herself in the mirror and was very happy with the new dress. Then we went back home and I have coke dinner. I coke the soy sauce shrimp and broccoli will clam my husband said delicious. I was very tired but I feel very happy.

10-11   On Tuesday with my daughter and mark went to beach to watch waves and birds. It was sunny very beautiful

10-14   I called my younger sister she talked to me about her wedding in December 3-95. Get marry. I with her very happy at afternoon I with my baby to Quincy market that magician made the balloons and gave my children. She was very happy.

After her first two weeks of instruction, Hung Mei completed a self-assessment form. She again reiterated the goal she had stated during her intake interview: "to know how to use the words in English better." The following writing sample, which Hung Mei composed as an introductory piece, provides a glimpse of her English literacy and language proficiency when she entered the project:

My name is Hung Mei. I born at 1966 DEC 9 in Chinese calendar. At here in 1967 January 19. I born in the Chinese year of the horse My name is my grandmother for me. The means red. Smile. The Hung means red and Mei is means smile. My last name inherited my father last name wu. My family and my friend usual call me a nickname Mei. Like my name. But I not fell special. Because in china most people like use Hung and Mei but with other noun together. At school I his a English name because we are learn English have English name. The name is do you like what kind name talk to teach. My English is Christian. I think the names very important for everyone need.

During her early weeks of participation, Hung Mei took advantage of every opportunity she had to advance toward her goal of improved English proficiency. She wrote daily, and, as in this example, almost always used her family experiences as the basis for writing:

> Today is my daughter seven month birthday at the afternoon. I bring my baby walking to the department store. I buy a pair of shoes for her. Because she is learning to stand and to walk everyday. The shoes are beautiful and the new fashion. My baby very much likes them. I hope my baby wears the shoes she feels curiosity and wonder and ignorance she thinks why do I have to wear shoes? I teach her that shoes will make the feet comfortable walking in winter shoes keep her feet warm. The shoes are a lifetime necessity for everyone. Tomorrow I hope my baby can stand up and walking.

Hung Mei also used her dialogue journal as an opportunity to advance her knowledge of English. In an early entry, she wrote to Ruth, a tutor who was her writing partner, of a conversation she had with her husband about his learning goals and of their joint interest in learning about "slang English." Her journal entry is displayed in Figure 3.8. Ruth responded with an explanation and a suggestion that Hung Mei and her husband compose a list of the words they would like to ask about (Figure 3.9), and the next day Hung Mei supplied a list that she and Ruth worked on together (Figure 3.10).

In response to reading, Hung Mei often reflected on life in the United States and commented on cultural differences:

> In America I think it's good if the family has children with parents living together. It is nice. Most children just live with the mother or father. The American people say they love the children. If the children like anything they will spend a lot of money to buy things. I think this is not too good. I would like to spend time to teach my children about helping other and to be good people.

Hung Mei was persistent in demanding that she be challenged each and every day and often used her reading response journal to evaluate the difficulty of the text the class had read:

> I like people working by own family store. The most customers was neighborhood friends. I think most people want self as boss. I didn't like the story. Too easy.

Hung Mei's final writing piece, which she chose to publish in the program's annual anthology, portrayed the remarkable progress she had made toward the lan-

FIGURE 3.8   Hung Mei's Dialogue Journal Entry

> Dear Ruth!   Nov – 8 – 95
>
> I'm very nice to meet you. Thank you
>
> for your help. I will always remember
>
> you. I hope we are journal to be
>
> Long Long tince.
>
>   Yesterday, I asked my Husband what
>
> do you want to pracice? His said,
>
> what is slang English. That also I want
>
> to know. Could you talk to me?
>   ﹏ – thanks, Ruth.
>   Chirstian wu.

guage proficiency goals she had set for herself. She received assistance from a tutor in punctuating this piece:

> I have a daughter and her name is Winger. I remember when I had the second child, my daughter with my husband came to the hospital to visit me. The first time she saw the little baby she felt shy and said "baby." She was only one year and nine months old. I told her to kiss him and told her that his name was Jeffrey, "he is your brother." For the first few months Winger was jealous of Jeffrey. Sometimes she just wanted to kiss him, but we worried she would be rough with him, so I said "No" all the time.

FIGURE 3.9   Ruth's Dialogue Journal Response to Hung Mei

> Dear Hung Mei,
>   Good for you for getting your husband involved in learning English! Slang is hard because it's different for different groups of people: my daughter comes home with expressions I've never heard... and it's not easy to guess 猜測 the meanings! ("Fresh," for example, which — at some point, with some kids — meant "terrific") Maybe he can start a list of slang words he hears that he doesn't know, and we'll try to find out. In fact, probably Richard could help us!
>   Do you have plans for Thanksgiving?
>   Your friend,
>   Ruth

Now it is better. Winger is almost three years old and Jeffrey is one year old. They play together. When Jeffrey rides a bike, Winger pushes him on the back. Winger feeds Jeffrey cereal. They listen to music, dance and turn around. They play dollies and put them to sleep. They take all the clothes out of the drawers and then laugh. It happens three times a day. One day Winger used Jeffrey as a foot stool to reach her clothes and they had a fashion show. When Winger is drawing, Jeffrey also wants to do it. When Jeffrey sits on my lap to watch TV, Winger wants to sit on my lap, too. They always want to do the same thing. Sometimes Jeffrey takes a

FIGURE 3.10 The Lesson that Followed the Dialogue

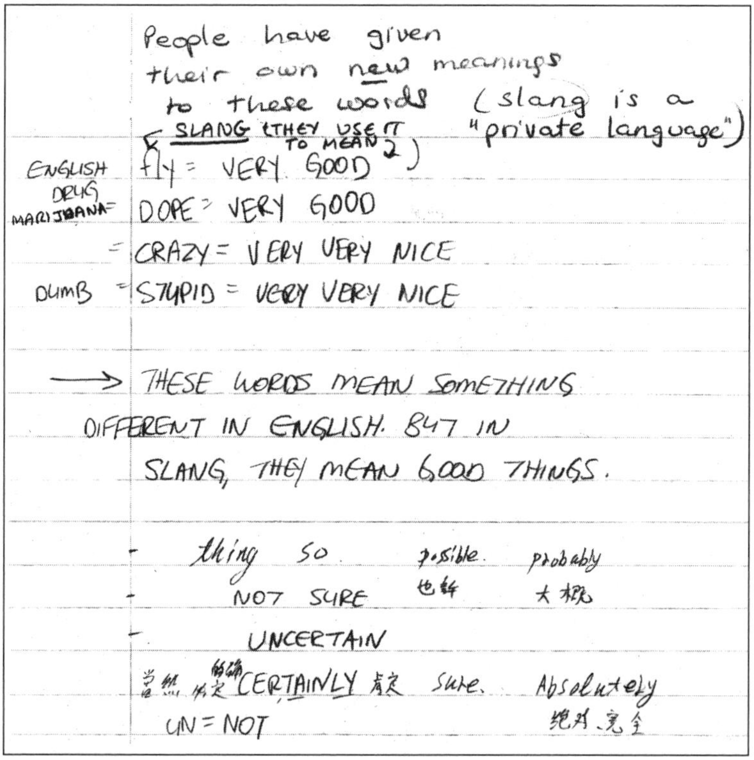
People have given
their own new meanings
to these words (slang is a
SLANG (THEY USE IT TO MEAN) "private language")
ENGLISH fly = VERY GOOD
DRUG MARIJUANA = DOPE = VERY GOOD
= CRAZY = VERY VERY NICE
DUMB = STUPID = VERY VERY NICE

→ THESE WORDS MEAN SOMETHING
DIFFERENT IN ENGLISH. BUT IN
SLANG, THEY MEAN GOOD THINGS.

- thing so possible. probably
- NOT SURE 也许 大概
- UNCERTAIN
当然 一定 的确 CERTAINLY 肯定 sure. Absolutely
UN = NOT 绝对、完全

nap and wakes up crying, and Winger says, "Can I hold him?" and hugs him and says "Don't cry, I love you." I ask her, "Is Jeffrey your best friend?" She said "Yes, he is my friend." Jeffrey always likes following his sister, but Winger sometimes wants to play alone, so she pushes him out and slams the door. She makes Jeffrey confused and that makes me mad, because I worried that her slamming the door may hurt Jeffrey's hand. Sometimes I watch them, and I feel very joyful. Winger and Jeffrey, I love you, babies.

While Hung Mei practiced her personal literacy in ILP classes, she continued to support her children's literacy development at home. She wrote to her daughter's teacher (Figure 3.11), asking for help in teaching Winger not to bite. She liked to share her own and her children's responses to the books they were reading, and she often completed reading response forms documenting what she or her husband read to the children and how they responded. An example is provided in Figure 3.12.

Her literacy log entries documented consistent and frequent parent-child literacy throughout her period of participation. During the final weeks, however, there was an evident shift in agency in the activities Hung Mei recorded, with her daughter,

FIGURE 3.11   Hung Mei's Letter to Her Daughter's Teacher

> Dear : Cathy   Sep - 24 - 86
>
> I'm winger MA'S mother. can you help me
> watch winger at school. I worry that she bite
> other kilds. because she is getting new teeth.
> Sometimes at home she bites me. can you help
> me teach her not to be like that. when you
> have any problem plese call me 884-5841.
>
>   sincerely.
>   Hung mei wu.

Winger, often taking the lead in initiating literacy events. These two examples are representative:

4-2-97   In the morning Winger want me to turn on the radio for her. Winger go to carry her baby and sit down the floor reading a book for her baby

5-2-97   Yesterday Winger pick up the letter want to put on the door for me teach her to read

After Hung Mei left the ILP, she secured a full-time job. She and her husband are now saving to buy their first house. Her daughter is now in her second year of Head Start. Preschool testing shows her to be achieving substantially above her age peers. Her son attends a local day care center. His teacher reported that he is achieving the benchmarks expected of the children in her class.

Silvia.   Silvia joined the ILP in October 1994, three months after she, her husband, and their three children arrived in the United States from Puerto Rico. Her daughter, Susanna, was nine years old and was enrolled in a bilingual fourth-grade classroom; her son, Octavio, was eight years old, and he was enrolled in a bilingual third-grade classroom. Her youngest child, Carlos, was six years old and enrolled in a bilingual first-grade classroom. Silvia had ten years of schooling in Puerto Rico, where she had, at one time, worked as a secretary in a hospital. When asked what she hoped to learn in

FIGURE 3.12   Hung Mei's Storybook Reading Response

Reading   Response

Name: _Hung mei WU_

Date: _9-27-96_

I read the book _What Do Toddlers Do ?_
(title of book)

with _Winger MA_
(name of child)

This is what happened when we shared the book:

Because this book is for Winger age. She saw the picture. The kids do something Like her self self. but she felt herself older. She called the Toddlers Baby. Baby. When her father read the book with her. she vere a quiet to listen. Winger Love thes book.

the program, Silvia said, "Everything!" and specifically mentioned her desire to learn to speak, understand, write, and read in English. She described her English proficiency as moderate, and after only one month in the program, she chose to try to write in English in class daily. Silvia remained in the program for two years. During this time her family life was disrupted by two serious events. A fire left the family temporarily homeless, and two of her children, Susanna and Octavio, were injured in a car accident.

At the time of enrollment, Silvia was very attentive to her children's schooling. During her intake interview, she reported that she monitored her children's homework every day by asking about it and helping with completion. In addition, because she walked her children to and from school, she had frequent opportunities to talk with their teachers, and she reported that she did so at least once a week. She and her children never visited the library, but she did read to them a few times each week from books that she had at home.

Throughout Silvia's three-year period of participation, her literacy logs documented daily attention to homework and storybook reading. She consistently noted which child she helped, the particular type of homework activity, the language of the homework task, and the titles of the books she read. The log presented in Figure 3.13 represents a typical series of log entries.

During a discussion in which Silvia reflected on the influence of the ILP on her interactions with her children, she explained that the amount of reading she did with her children had not changed but that the ways they read books had changed. She said that she had learned particularly to take time to have her children reread stories to her after she had read to them.

At each opportunity to self-assess and reformulate her goals, Silvia reiterated her interest in improving her oral and written English. Her goal was always a variation of the following statement: "I would like to do better. pronounce the words better . . . I want to write much better in English." She often evaluated her work on the basis of the language in which she composed: "I like wrote about the pilgrims. And also wrote in my journal because I wrote in English." In the middle of the second year, her goal remained focused on language learning but was explicitly aimed at preparing herself for employment opportunities: "I want to learn English to take the G.E.D. and I can get the training of computer or typing so that I can look for a job. Because I always wanted to be a secretary."

Silvia's work showed steady advancement toward her goal of improved written English. In class, she often chose to write about family members, frequently her mother and grandmother. Two pieces about her mother document the progress she made in writing. The first was written within her first two weeks of enrollment, and the latter was written toward the end of her second year. Each piece was composed without assistance:

> Her name is Elba Letriz, think I what herself debit the feeling sad because she birthday in november nine. And my grandmother what is herself mother died in november 10, 1993. Moreover, she to suffer much when I and my children us separated that she crying for two days and when speak herself feeling a little sad. Because in Puerto Rico always walking together us visited all them day all but us to call for telephone. (October 1994)

> Her name is Elba Letriz. I remember that she always were with us. When we going to sleep she would sing a song to us. She is short. She wore pants, blouse, dress, and skirt, too. My mother is very important to me because she's my mother as well as my best friend. I remember when I came home from school she would help us with are homework. (March 1996)

On leaving the program, Silvia was asked if she had made progress toward her goals. Her unedited written response documented her growth in language learning:

FIGURE 3.13   Silvia's Literacy Log

LITERACY LOG

NAME: Holy

MONTH: March

DATE	Reading, Writing, Viewing and Talking Activities I Shared with My Child or Children	CHILD'S NAME AND AGE
3-21-96	Yesterday, I helped my daughter Suleika with "homework of math.	
3-26-96	Yesterday I helped my daughter Suleika with homework of social study. Also my son Christopher read a book to me the title is cirindá.	
3-27-96	Yesterday, we went to my friend's home. Yesterday, I helped my son Oscar with homework of math.	
April 1st 96	Yesterday, I went with my husband, my children and my friend and her children to the park. After we went to my friend's home. Last night I helped my son Oscar with a homework of English.	
4-3-96	Last night, I read a book to my children the title is my friends.	
4-4-96	Last night, I helped to my son Christopher with a homework of Spanish.	
4-8-96	Yesterday, we went to my friend's home. Also we played card.	
4-9-96	Yesterday, my son Christopher read a book to me the title is "El dolor de muelas"	
4-11-96	Last night, my son Christopher read a book to me the title is Pippo. My daughter Suleika, my son Oscar and my son Christopher spoke with my aunt on the telephone from P.R.	

I can read, write and speak English. Also, I can understand many words. I can read books, and when I received letters in English I can read and understand.

As for Silvia's children, we learned that their experiences in school could not be predicted on the basis of their mother's involvement with their learning. During Silvia's first year in the program, we obtained permission to talk with the classroom teachers of two of Silvia's children, Susanna and Octavio, and to review their school records. Susanna, the fourth-grader, was generally very successful. Her teacher described her as a "prolific writer in Spanish; she gets her ideas down, then revises and edits." She also said that she wrote "more in her journal than any other student in the class." Susanna's report card grades were consistent with her teacher's comments. In Spanish reading, she received 3 As and a B for the four marking periods. In English reading, she received an A for the first marking period, Bs for the second and third periods, and a B– for the final period. In English language, her grades were A, B, A–, and B over the four quarters. In Spanish language, she received three As and a B throughout the year.

Unlike Susanna, Octavio met with considerable difficulty in his third-grade classroom. His teacher reported that at the beginning of the school year he could not read or write at all and did not know the alphabet. He had been referred to the child study team, the first step in identifying students for special education services, although no apparent action had been taken. Silvia was aware that her son was far behind other third-graders and stated that he was not taught "enough" in Puerto Rico and consequently arrived in third grade unable to read and write:

> *Lo que pasa es que él este en Puerto Rico no le enseñaron lo suficiente a él porque él ya está en el tercer grado y él no lee como él debe leer y no escribe como debe de escribir.*

> What happens is that he, in Puerto Rico they did not teach him enough because he is now in the third grade and he does not read how he should and he does not write how he should write. . . . Because he reads in syllables.

Silvia worked hard to support Octavio in school, helping with homework and reading and writing with him daily. His teacher reported that Silvia was in the classroom "all the time" seeking strategies for helping Octavio and commented on the positive role she played in his learning: "She deserves credit for what he has accomplished—a team effort."

By the end of the school year, Octavio's teacher reported that he had improved in reading and writing but was still far below grade level. His report cards documented the difficulty he had experienced. In all areas relating to written language, he received marks indicating that he is weak or making inconsistent progress. In reading, his only clear progress was in the area of active participation. In speaking and listening, Octavio received the grade of P ("progressing") for his participation in discussions and clear expression of ideas. For work habits and conduct, Octavio was rated I ("inconsistent").

Summarizing the case studies.   The three case studies are representative of the many different learners the ILP has served since its inception. They differ from one another in many ways—in years in the United States, ethnicities, languages, formal schooling, and family circumstances. Perhaps of greater interest are two critical commonalities—the parents' persistence in advancing their own learning and their dedication to their children's learning. When we examine the individual cases—those presented here and the literally hundreds more that we have in our files—we are struck by how much is new in the lives of each family member and therefore how much they must learn: new housing, new schooling, new language, new babies, new friends, new jobs, new laws. We are also struck by the number of serious distractions they have—securing housing and food, combating neighborhood crime and sometimes spousal abuse, caring for their own and their children's health and sometimes that of older family members, and maintaining contact with family and friends miles away. We are impressed by their ability to negotiate what would seem to many to be overwhelming obstacles in ways that allow time in a typical day to dedicate to their own and their children's learning.

Summary of the Evidence

During the ten years that the ILP has been in operation, it has served primarily new immigrants, most having lived in the United States for five years or less. Participants arrive from many different countries and speak many different first languages, but most are Latino and most speak Spanish as a first language. The typical parent has completed approximately eight years of schooling in her own country and has chosen to enroll in the ILP to advance her own learning and to support her children's success in American schools.

Over the years of the project, we have used a diverse collection of assessment practices to monitor and document its outcomes. We have examined attendance and retention, writing progress, parents' personal uses of reading and writing, parents' engagement of their children in literacy activities, and children's success in school. Documentation has included self-reported data; reading and writing samples; interviews with parents, teachers, and children; questionnaires completed by parents and teachers; and school records. The findings from the various data sources are summarized as follows:

1. During its ten years of implementation, the ILP achieved rates of attendance and retention that exceed those of traditional adult basic education and, in many cases, of other family literacy programs, indicating that daily instructional practices are effective in maintaining parents' motivation to advance their own and their children's literacy knowledge.
2. From beginning to end of their program participation, parents increased their use of reading and writing outside class to achieve personal goals, thereby making print literacy a more frequent routine in their daily lives.
3. From beginning to end of their program participation, parents increased the frequency with which they engaged their children in the types of literacy events

that have been found to prepare children for success in early reading, particularly, and in school, generally.

4. By the end of program participation, 80 percent of parents reported engaging children in storybook reading at least once each week, a practice that has been found to correlate highly with early reading achievement. This rate of participation in storybook reading represents a substantial increase from the level reported on entry to the project.

5. At the beginning of the parents' program participation, teachers and parents reported that, on average, the children of the parents who participated had good attitudes toward school and learning and were average or above-average academic achievers. At the end of the program, children maintained or slightly improved both their attitudes toward school and learning and their rates of academic performance.

6. In the case of children who struggle in school, their difficulty appears to be related to an array of complex factors, including learning disability, transience, divorce, and ineffective schooling, rather than to the single factor of parent involvement in their education.

Up to this point, the discussion has focused on program practices and outcomes as they relate to parents and their children. In the next chapter, the focus turns from the ways the program influences how parents learn to use literacy alone and with their children to the ways parents learn to use literacy to mediate their interactions with their children's classroom teachers.

NOTES

1. The retention rate was calculated on the basis of the number of parents who completed the full instructional cycle after remaining for at least two weeks. The two-week minimum stay criterion was based on our observation that learners who leave during the first two weeks generally do so not because of poor program quality but rather because of an inadequate program match. For example, often they are learners whose primary purpose is to acquire English fluency, rather than English literacy and, as a result, the reading and writing activities that are part of the program are of low interest to them.

4 Bringing Parents and Teachers Together to Help Children Learn

The evidence is now beyond dispute. When schools work together with families to support learning, children tend to succeed not just in school, but throughout life.
—Henderson and Berla, 1994, p. 1

As Henderson and Berla suggest, few question the importance of parent involvement in their children's eventual success in school. So widespread is the belief that parents play an integral role in their children's school success that, in 1996, in his annual State of American Education Address, U.S. Secretary of Education Richard Riley called on parents to make it their "patriotic duty to find an extra thirty minutes every day to help their children learn more" (Office of Governmental and Interagency Affairs, 1996). Despite this "call to duty," many teachers believe that parents are essentially failing to uphold their end of the deal. For example, in a survey of 1,000 public school teachers conducted by the organization Public Agenda, only 27 percent said that parental involvement in their school is high, and 66 percent gave parents fair or poor ratings on involvement with their children's education. Most teachers (83 percent) believed that many parents are failing to meet obligations such as creating structure and setting limits, monitoring TV viewing and video games, and holding their children accountable for behavior and academic performance (Farkas, Johnson, Duffett, Aulicino, & McHugh, 1999). Majorities of both suburban (67 percent) and urban (82 percent) teachers reported that too many parents have little sense of what is going on with their children's education. Nearly seven in ten teachers indicated that "the most serious problem they face is with students who try to get by doing as little work as possible" (p. 25), and they blame parents for this behavior.

The data from parents in the same survey, however, do not support teachers' beliefs that they are disengaged from their children's education. Rather, 51 percent said they worry more about the quality of their children's education than they do about other contemporary social pressures, such as the threat of crime or drugs or economic security; 73 percent reported that their concern about their child's education determined the community in which they chose to live; 56 percent said they spoke with the principal or teachers before their child enrolled in their current school; 33 percent checked with other parents to see which teachers would be best. Three-quarters of respondents believed that they are more involved in their children's education than their own parents were.

In spite of these differences, there is an important point of agreement in the survey. Both parents and teachers agree that whatever the level of individual involvement, parents, in general, need to become *more* involved in their children's education. But when parents and teachers speak of parent involvement, what do they actually mean? Are they always talking about the same thing? And what do we know about effective ways to support parent involvement?

The term *parent involvement* has become a sort of catchall. Teachers often determine a parent's involvement in their children's education on the basis of how often they *see* the parent—their presence at school meetings, on field trips, or at fund-raisers. In contrast, parents often judge their involvement on the basis of the actions they take at home and out of the teacher's sight, such as preparing children for school, monitoring homework, or encouraging good behavior. A review of the published literature indicates that parent involvement is used to encompass all of these activities. More far-reaching than family literacy, which relates to parents' and children's literacy and language activities in relation to any aspect of their lives, parent involvement is used to refer to activities that have a direct relationship to children's experiences in school. As defined by Hoover-Dempsey and Sandler (1997), parent involvement includes:

> Home-based activities related to children's learning in school—for example, reviewing the child's work and monitoring child progress, helping with homework, discussing school events or course issues with the child, providing enrichment activities pertinent to school success, and talking by phone with the teacher. They also include school-based involvement, focused on such activities as driving on a field trip, staffing a concession booth at school games, coming to school for scheduled conferences or informal conversations, volunteering at school, serving on a parent–teacher advisory board. (p. 6)

Scholars of parent involvement (e.g., Comer, 1984, 1986, Epstein, 1986, 1994; Epstein & Dauber, 1991; Hoover-Dempsey & Sandler, 1997; Lareau, 1987, 1989) indicate that there are two particular issues that influence the parent involvement decisions parents make. One is parents' perceptions of their roles and responsibilities; the other is teachers' actions in inviting and helping parents to become a part of their children's education.

Parents' Perceptions of Roles and Responsibilities

There is ample evidence that the ways parents perceive their roles and responsibilities in relation to their children's schooling vary by ethnic and socioeconomic groups. For example, in her study of middle- and low-socioeconomic families, Lareau (1987, 1989) found that working-class parents had a "separated" view of home and school. They tended to believe that their roles involved getting children ready for school—making certain that they were courteous, respectful, and prompt—but did not believe that their roles included helping children learn. This perception contrasted sharply with that of middle-class parents, who saw education as a "shared enterprise and scrutinized, monitored, and supplemented the school experience of their children" (1987, p. 81). Other studies have reported results largely similar to Lareau's. In a sample of 95 Mexican American parents selected to represent both low- and middle-socioeconomic groups, Parra and Henderson (1982) found that only two parents indicated that both the home and the school were responsible for fostering children's intellectual development or academic achievement, and both of these parents were from the middle-class sample. All others in the sample saw this responsibility as the sole province of the schools, whereas parents were responsible for monitoring children's attendance, behavior, health, and hygiene. Lynch and Stein (1987) studied a sample of 63 Latino parents whose children were in special education, a program that explicitly demands parent involvement. They also found them reluctant to raise questions about their children's academic programs, noting that they "spoke of the school and its programs respectfully" and indicated that they felt that "the teacher knows best" (p. 109). Delgado-Gaitan (1990) explained that the parents she studied "believed that the caring home environment which they create is one of the most important ways in which they can help their children" (p. 88).

Although there are certainly studies in which nonmainstream families take a view of their roles in relation to their children's learning that is closely aligned with that of middle-class parents (e.g., Clark, 1983; Segal, 1985), it is difficult to deny the presence of dissonance between parents' and teachers' expectations for parental actions in at least some households. The consequence of dissonance is that parents fail to perform the tasks that teachers perceive as an essential part of school success, and teachers conclude that parents are uninterested and uninvolved in their children's education. As explained by Galindo and Escamilla (1995), these parents "may define their role in a way that they and their children interpret as being supportive but which might be interpreted by school personnel as a lack of support because of the parent's absence from school activities" (p. 25).

The Importance of the Actions Teachers Take

Several have argued that when discontinuity in roles and responsibilities exists, teachers must explicitly teach parents how to assume new roles—that teachers must shift from "telling to showing nonmainstream parents" (Edwards, 1991, p. 211) what to do. This stance is consistent with Goldenberg's (1987) observation that the parents he studied were capable and willing to help their children but that there was no systematic attempt by the school to help them do so. This observation was supported by results of a study by Epstein (1986), who found that 58 percent of parents reported rarely or never receiving requests from the teacher to be involved in learning activities at home. More recently, it received support in Cuckle's (1996) report that parents were "willing to help, but lacked confidence in their abilities. They want advice from the expert teachers, and were dissatisfied with what was offered" (p. 30).

The importance of the actions teachers take to support parent involvement is evident in several studies. Epstein (1986) investigated parent involvement among two groups of parents: those whose children's teachers were regarded by their principals as leaders in parent involvement and those whose children's teachers were not. She identified 12 parent involvement practices, clustered within five categories: techniques that involve reading and books; techniques that encourage discussions between parents and children; techniques based on informal activities and games that use common materials at home; techniques based on formal contracts among parents, teachers, and children; and techniques that involve tutoring and teaching the child in skills and drills. Parents whose children's teachers were regarded as leaders in parent involvement reported significantly more frequent use of 9 of the 12 parent involvement practices. Epstein concluded that the actions teachers take are critical in influencing both the type and the frequency of parents' school-related interactions with their children.

Further, Epstein found that teachers who were considered leaders in parent involvement held similar expectations for parents with both high and low levels of education and that both groups of parents engaged in similar activities with their children. Conversely, teachers who were not regarded as leaders in parent involvement viewed parents with little education as not capable of helping their children with learning activities at home and rarely sought their help or support. Such views in essence limit parents' opportunities to learn about school and conflict with evidence that parents increase their understanding about school most when the teacher frequently uses parent involvement practices and when the teacher frequently communicates with the family (Epstein, 1986).

Cochran and Dean (1991) studied the effects of a systematic, explicit, and broad-based program for supporting parent involvement, which, in part, included a series of activities for parents designed to build both confidence and skills specific to active involvement with the child's school and teacher. In addition to identifying information that they hoped to share with parents, they also made an assumption that there was much for them to learn from the community: "We assumed that much of the most useful knowledge about the rearing of children can be found in the community itself—in the older generations, in social networks, and in ethnic and cultural traditions . . ." (p. 262). They found their approach to be successful: children in the participating families did better in first grade than children from similar backgrounds in a comparison group. This difference was strongest for children with the least-educated parents.

Comer (1984) implemented a comprehensive school reform model in which parents were an essential part of the school community, participating both as part of the governance and management body and also as part of a parent–aide program, in which they had opportunities to both provide and receive support in school skills and experiences. Comer reported that the presence of parents as meaningful members of the school community resulted in improving the climate of the school, reducing behavior problems, and supporting academic achievement and motivation. As well, reduced conflict and increased hope and confidence permitted staff and curriculum development and improved teaching and learning. Further, Comer reported that the benefits of the parent involvement program accrued to adults as well as children:

> Many of the parents associated with our school program became mobilized psychologically, acquired skills and confidence, and returned to school or took jobs to which they feel they would not have aspired or would not have been able to hold prior to their involvement in the school program. (p. 335)

Evident in the work of Cochran and Dean (1991) and Comer (1984) is an emphasis on reciprocity, defined by Davies (1996) as the practice of establishing clear relationships and mutual obligations between all the parts of the child's world. Similarly, the work of Moll and his colleagues (Moll, Amanti, Neff, & Gonzalez, 1992; Gonzalez et al., 1995; Vélez-Ibánez & Greenberg, 1992) has emphasized the critical importance of assuming a reciprocal learning stance when initiating parent involvement efforts:

> Reciprocal practices establish serious obligations based on the assumption of "confianza" (mutual trust), which is reestablished or confirmed with each exchange, and leads to the development of long-term relationships. Each exchange with relatives, friends, and neighbors entails not only many practical activities . . . but constantly provides contexts where learning can occur—contexts, for example, where children have ample opportunities to participate in activities with people they trust. (Moll et al., 1992, p. 134)

The potential of this approach for having a positive influence on the ways teachers perceive and interact with parents is evident in a journal entry made by one of the participating teachers:

> As I reread some of the early journal entries I made for this project, I realize how I have changed my views of the households. As I read these entries, I realized that I had discussed my students in terms of low academics, home-life problems, alienation, and SES, and that I was oriented toward a deficit model. I no longer see the families I visited that way. Since I am looking for resources, I am finding resources, and I recognized the members of the families for who they are, and for their talents and unique personalities. We now have a reciprocal relationship where we exchange goods, services, and information. (Gonzalez et al., 1995, p. 461)

Despite these particularly noteworthy initiatives, relatively few schools have established approaches to parent involvement that can boast meaningful success, and the consequences of failure should not be underestimated. As early as 1974, Getzels argued that the consequence of failing to recognize discontinuities between home and school "is to place the children and their schools at a severe disadvantage in relation to other children and other schools" (p. 224). A quarter-century later, in many classrooms, few inroads have been made. In a study of how teachers and students connected home and school literacy practices, McCarthey (1997) concluded that, in the classrooms she studied, despite teachers' first steps to welcome diversity, the practices in place "reinforced middle-class literacy values while inadvertently ignoring or devaluing (mostly through lack of knowledge) literacy practices in non-middle-class homes" (p. 147).

Some claim that the primary reason that efforts have not taken hold is because emphasis is placed on transmitting ideas and information to parents, rather than on transforming the ideas of both parents and teachers (Swap, 1993). Shockley, Michalove, and Allen (1995) argue that such efforts are based on a program rather than a partnership model and, as such, are doomed to failure:

> Programs are implemented; partnerships are developed. Programs are adopted; partnerships are constructed. Parent involvement programs as America's schools have implemented them have serious problems. By their very nature, most programs have steps, elements or procedures that become static. A program cannot constantly reinvent itself, change each year, be different in every classroom, and for every teacher–family–child relationship. Yet schools and parents have a shared and vested interest in children that almost demands some kind of collaboration. We believe, along with an increasing number of home and school educators, that this shared responsibility should be a genuine partnership. (p. 91)

The home–school partnership initiatives that have worked are distinguished by some very clear and consistent characteristics. First, at their foundation, there is an underlying respect for parents—an assumption that they are very much concerned with their children's academic success and interested in collaborating with teachers in ways that will support their children in school. Second, there is an understanding that different family cultures, traditions, and circumstances may dictate different ways of collaborating. Third, they each share an assumption that parents and teachers have much to learn from each other, and they have established practices and routines that enable such learning to occur. Fourth, there is an understanding that parents may need some explicit instruction in the types of activities teachers believe will benefit children, and teachers take explicit and frequent actions to provide adequate support to parents. Fifth, there is an understanding that connecting all aspects of children's lives will enhance children's opportunities to learn, and emphasis is placed on using children's home and community learning experiences at least partially as the basis for classroom learning experiences.

Acting on the Evidence: Home–School Partnerships and the Intergenerational Literacy Project

From the start, the purpose of the ILP was to influence both the ways parents shared literacy with their children at home and the ways parents learned to interact with teachers at school. But despite our conversations and our good intentions, we found that establishing the groundwork for meaningful collaboration between parents and teachers was very difficult to do. In the early years of the project, we were located in a community center several blocks from any of the elementary schools, and we reasoned that our location explained the difficulty. But by the fourth year of the project, we were sharing a corridor with elementary school children and their teachers. Yet, two years later, we had made few inroads into establishing routines or practices that could be expected to bring parents into meaningful partnerships with the school community. At school, administrators and teachers were always kind and cordial to ILP parents and teachers. However, they asked few questions about what we were doing or about how we might all work together. Information we sent to teachers and administrators identifying children as project participants went largely unnoticed. Indeed, at a meeting called to talk about the ways the ILP might collaborate with the rest of the school community, principals reacted with surprise when we reported that such information had been sent. As well, on those occasions when we had informal conversations with teachers about ways that parents participating in the ILP might be involved in classroom activities, we learned that many teachers believed that parents with limited English proficiency were limited in the ways they could support their children's academic learning or participate in classrooms.

As for parents, they routinely reported being intimidated by administrators and teachers and confused by or misinformed about the experiences their children were having in school. Many reported that although they carefully monitored their children's school activities, they seldom went to school. Rather, they asked their children questions, monitored their homework, made certain they attended school each day, and made certain the children were clean, rested, and well behaved.

So, it seemed, the actions we had put in place during the early years of the project to support parent–teacher interactions—discussing with parents the types of questions to ask of teachers, informing teachers of the ILP and the families who were participating, suggesting ways teachers might build on the activities parents were practicing with their children at home—had very little effect. As we considered these circumstances against the backdrop of evidence about the importance of parent involvement in children's school achievement, we were certain that we had to do more to influence the ways parents and teachers interacted. Two particular projects, the Parents as Classroom Storybook Readers Project and the Home–School Portfolio Project, grew out of this commitment. In each case, as we designed the projects, we were mindful of the characteristics of effective initiatives derived from the research.

Parents as Classroom Storybook Readers Project

The purpose of the Parents as Classroom Storybook Readers Project (Krol-Sinclair, 1996; Paratore & Krol-Sinclair, 1996) was to help parents enter into partnerships with teachers by bringing into the classroom what they were learning to do at home—shared storybook reading. We know that reliability is important to classroom teachers, who must squeeze many different activities into a typical school day, and so we invited participation only from parents who had demonstrated dependability through high attendance rates at the ILP. Parents were paired with bilingual classroom teachers who volunteered to have them read in their classrooms. The classrooms in which parents read were not necessarily those attended by their own children, but rather any bilingual classroom where teachers were interested in having parents participate as storybook readers.

The project had two essential components: training sessions and classroom read-aloud sessions. The 30- to 60-minute training sessions occurred either the day of or the day before each classroom visit. At these sessions, parents previewed and practiced the books they would read aloud, and they were introduced to and practiced particular read-aloud strategies.

We collected data on outcomes during the first two years of the project. During the first year, the mothers who participated had relatively high levels of education (all had completed at least two years of high school); during the second year, the parents who participated had fewer than seven years of formal schooling.

What parents did.   At each 30–60-minute training session, parents met with the project director to select a book and to prepare to read it in the classroom. Parents were provided a selection of books in Spanish and English from which to choose. They were reminded of the read-aloud strategies that had been introduced in their ILP classes, such as engaging children in prediction, engaging children through thoughtful questioning, and guiding story retellings. The session leader often demonstrated and modeled the way she would read a particular book to a classroom full of children rather to an individual as the parents had previously learned to do, and parents had the opportunity to rehearse by reading aloud to the group.

Classroom visits generally took about a half hour. At the beginning of the session, students were usually seated on a rug in a book corner, and the parent sat or stood in the front of the classroom. The parents used big books for reading the story with the class. They began each session by showing the children the book cover and reading the title and the author's name. They asked students to comment on the title or illustrations presented on the book cover and to make predictions about what they thought would happen in the story. Each student's suggestion was acknowledged.

During the reading of the story, parents invited participation from students, building on their comments and answering questions as they arose. Many of the books chosen (e.g., *Here Comes the Cat, Una extraña visita*) were repetitive and predictable, and parents encouraged students to say the words along with the reader.

After reading the book, parents asked the students to retell the story, using a variety of methods. Some parents routinely paged through the book a second time, inviting comments about each picture and occasionally asking questions about what was happening, how the characters felt, and so forth. Other parents focused on narrative structure, asking students about the setting, problem, solution, and consequence of the story. Invariably, parents asked the students what they liked about the story. Before leaving, the parents gave the teacher several small copies of the book for the children to read to themselves over the following week.

Following each reading session, the parent met briefly with the literacy teacher to discuss how the read-aloud had gone and the students' reactions to the book. The literacy teacher provided feedback and, when appropriate, suggestions for the next read-aloud session.

What teachers did.   After introducing the parent to the class, teachers participated by observing the session and occasionally offering comments during the read-aloud.

What we learned. Because the Parents as Classroom Storybook Readers Project was a new initiative, we systematically collected data that would help us determine whether it was beneficial to participants and worthy of teachers', parents', and children's time and effort. Among the data sources were the project director's field notes of the training sessions, audiotapes of the classroom read-aloud sessions, interviews with parents, interviews with classroom teachers, and audiotapes of parent–child storybook reading sessions at home. As reported by Krol-Sinclair (1996) and Paratore and Krol-Sinclair (1996), the data indicated several important and positive outcomes. First, both parents and teachers perceived the read-aloud sessions as beneficial to the students. Parents described the children as enthusiastic, eager to participate, and imaginative in their responses. One teacher's response was representative of many; she said that the parent was helping to "stimulate the [children's] minds and to help them be more intelligent and get good grades." Teachers also noted the positive influence on children, perhaps best exemplified in one teacher's comment: "It was exciting to have one of the children's mothers read to my students. I'm sure it will inspire other youngsters to go home and invite their parents to do the same." All of the participating teachers said they wanted the parents to visit their classrooms more frequently and to participate more actively in their children's education.

Second, when reading aloud to children in the classroom, parents not only used the strategies in which they had been trained but also relied on their personal read-aloud styles and behaviors. That is, some encouraged children to repeat repetitive phrases after them, and others routinely paused to let children predict the next word or phrase; some engaged children by asking questions along the way, and others did so by drawing children's attention to illustrations. The mixing and matching of their personal read-aloud behaviors with the strategies taught in the sessions prevented the read-aloud sessions from seeming scripted. Rather, parents wove new strategies in with their existing practices.

Third, parents used strategies they had learned and practiced in classroom storybook reading sessions when reading with their children at home. Audiotapes of parent-child read-alouds at home indicated that parents engaged their children in home reading sessions in a more interactive manner than they had previously. Of importance, their work in classrooms led them to challenge their own children to engage in what they believed to be new and difficult tasks, and they often found their children to be more capable than they had believed. One participant shared the following example:

> When I took the book home last night I showed my nephew the cover and read him the title and asked him what he thought the book was about. He said, "The tree wants leaves." I was very surprised that he could make a prediction like that. When we read the book, he was happy because the tree got leaves.

Fourth, participating in classrooms as storybook readers provided parents with an opportunity to learn about the culture of American schools and classrooms. Prior to this project, most of the parents had visited their children's classrooms only to transport their children to or from school or to participate in a parent–teacher conference or formal meeting. The storybook reading project provided many of them with their first extended look at a classroom in session. Several noted the contrast between their observations and their previous experiences with schools in their own countries. A comment made by one mother was representative of many:

> I never saw a class like that before. All of the children were doing different things, and they were all having fun, but they were learning. When I first came in, I thought this is not good, it is not school, but I saw that the children were learning and I think that it's good.

After participating in the classroom read-alouds, the parents were able to articulate classroom routines, describe the types of print experiences children have in school, and discuss how children learn to read in school. Participating in the classroom as storybook readers provided a context in which parents could acquire "classroom literacy" (Corno, 1989).

Fifth, teachers gained insight into the capacity of parents with limited formal schooling and limited English proficiency to support children's literacy development. As one teacher noted, "Even though her English isn't perfect, this mother reads with a great deal of expression and got the children to say the words along with her." Teachers remarked in similar ways on the literacy strategies parents used during storybook reading sessions and their students' resulting involvement throughout the story. One teacher commented:

> The parent kept the students involved by encouraging participation in identifying pictures and colors. As the story progressed, the students were identifying the pictures and colors without first being asked. When the story was over, the parent was interested in whether the children enjoyed the story. She encouraged responses from the students as to what parts of the story they enjoyed.

In the end, teachers came to view the project as one more strategy in their repertoire for helping children become successful readers, and importantly, they came to see parents as valuable partners in that endeavor.

Home-School Literacy Portfolio

The Home-School Literacy Portfolio Project[1] was planned to achieve two particular purposes. First, by teaching parents to document children's literacy activities at home, we hoped we would increase their awareness of their children's literacy learning and of the roles they might play in it. Second, by teaching parents to share the portfolio with teachers, we hoped we would increase teachers' awareness of the ways children use literacy at home and of the ways parents and teachers might work together to teach children to read and write. There were two essential components to the project: the construction of a home literacy portfolio and the sharing of the portfolio during parent–teacher conferences. We collected data on outcomes during four years of the project.

What parents did.   During their adult literacy classes, parents were taught how to observe their children's uses of literacy at home and were introduced to the idea of documenting their children's uses of literacy outside school by collecting samples of their activities and saving them in home literacy portfolios. They discussed the types of materials to collect, and emphasis was placed on the importance of including both samples of children's written work (for example, drawings, stories, letters) and their own written observations. For example, in one class, on the day the portfolio project was introduced, teachers asked learners why it might be important to keep a portfolio. Parents' responses were recorded on the semantic map as presented in Figure 4.1.

Once each week, parents were asked to share examples from their children's family literacy portfolios with other members of their ILP class. These sharing sessions were very interactive. As parents showed and described portfolio artifacts, teachers and learners questioned and commented. Often a particular presentation elicited applause. Field notes recorded by one of the adult literacy teachers during a sharing session help us to understand what parents did at home and what they said during the sharing sessions. One teacher recorded the following:

> Today, many learners brought portfolios. First Nubia shared, telling us about the book she read, *Green Leaf, Yellow Leaf.* She showed us a poster Walter [her child] made. . . . Then everyone watched as Nubia shared the birthday card her son made for his father. It was a collage. Ana Maria [a teacher] commented on the opportunity to use a birthday card as an opportunity to use writing to express feelings. . . . Then Marie Louise shared Kelvin's drawings. She mostly just held them up and showed them. Graciela commented that it looked like he was drawing shapes. Roxana shared next about what she did with her nephew. . . . She showed the board book she read and made the noises and people in the class laughed. Then she showed a drawing Anthony made. . . . Marta showed a picture Brenda drew of her mother and another picture . . . then Marta

FIGURE 4.1   Parents' Perceptions of the Purposes of a Family Literacy Portfolio

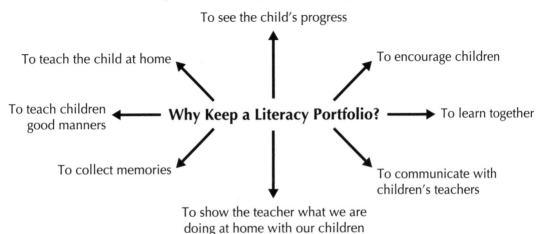

shared a cereal box entry form that Brenda filled out. . . . When Marta goes to work Brenda leaves her notes and pictures that say I love you. Ana Maria [a teacher] pointed out that children of different ages do different things, but it's all important.

Additionally, parents were taught strategies for sharing their children's family literacy portfolios with teachers during informal meetings and in parent–teacher conferences. During class, parents were provided short articles about parent–teacher conferences to read and discuss. Notes from one teacher described a typical class:

> I asked the class to talk in small groups about three questions: What is the teacher's role in education? What are the parents' roles in education? Why are parent-teacher conferences important? . . . The students divided in 5 tables. . . . They shared lots of information and examples . . . after 15 minutes, each table shared the answers with the whole class. I made a list of the answers on the blackboard. After this, we read the booklet, "Your Parent–Teacher Conference."

The teacher recorded that on the following day, the focus shifted to the particular questions parents might ask of teachers during a conference and to particular ways they might share and discuss the artifacts within their children's portfolios. The teaching team presented a role play of a typical conference, with one teacher assuming the role of parent and the other of teacher. Following the role play, the teachers summarized the points they hoped parents would remember:

- Introduce yourself.
- Be on time.
- Be prepared—you only have a short time to talk.
- Bring portfolio and ask if you can share it with the teacher.
- Let the teacher know that you are willing to communicate with her. (Ask if you can contact her when you need to.)
- Remember that here [in the United States] teachers expect parents to help at home.
- Write down what you want to talk about.

Activities such as these—sharing and discussing portfolio artifacts, discussing and preparing for parent–teacher conferences—continued each week throughout the course of parents' participation in the ILP.

What teachers were asked to do.   Classroom teachers were invited to attend a series of three after-school seminars during which they read and discussed key texts and articles about family literacy and about establishing and supporting home–school partnerships. (The texts and articles read are presented in Appendix D.) The meetings provided a forum to discuss the ways the ideas they read about applied to their own community and to the families of the children they taught. Teachers also learned about the home literacy portfolios being assembled by families participating in the ILP. Central to the discussions was the use of routine parent–teacher conferences as opportunities for parents and teachers to pool their knowledge of children's developing literacy and to use their shared knowledge to continue to support family literacy and children's academic learning. Teachers were asked to encourage parents to bring the portfolios to parent–teacher conferences and to provide time during the conference for parents to share the portfolios and to discuss the child's uses of literacy at home.

At the end of each seminar, teachers were asked to take a specific action. For example, following the first seminar, during which teachers read and discussed a brief, three-page section from Guadelupe Valdés's *Con Respeto*, they were asked to do the following during the three weeks before the next seminar:

> Read all of *Con Respeto*. Reflect on it. What surprised you? What didn't? What did you agree with? Disagree with? What are the implications for your interactions with parents and children?
>
> Consider and implement a strategy for working in a collaborative relationship with at least one family to help you learn more about the ways family members use literacy during their daily routines. Describe what you did and what you learned.

When they returned the next week, they shared and discussed their responses to their reading and their subsequent actions and interactions with parents. Then the "read, reflect, respond, and action" cycle began again, with teachers focused on a new focal text and new ideas for building home–school partnerships. This format was followed at each seminar.

What we learned.   As in the Parents as Classroom Storybook Readers Project, the Home–School Portfolio Project was a new initiative, one that demanded time and attention from parents, teachers, and children. As such, we were interested in formally investigating its outcomes to determine if it was effective in helping parents and teachers to collaborate in supporting children's literacy development. To do so, we conducted a series of studies (Paratore et al., 1995; Paratore, Hindin, Krol-Sinclair, & Durán, 1999; Paratore, Hindin, Krol-Sinclair, Durán, & Emig, 1999) and collected evidence from a total of 24 parent–teacher dyads. Data included a series of individual interviews with parents and teachers at the start of the project and immediately after parent–teacher conferences, audiotapes from the conferences, and copies of the home literacy portfolios. We learned some important lessons about the potential of home literacy portfolios to positively shape interactions between parents and teachers.

First, transcript data indicated that the conversation during the conference was generally friendly and collaborative: parents and teachers used the portfolio artifacts to build on and reinforce the other's point of view. The practice of validating or confirming what was said was reciprocal between parents and teachers—teachers affirmed parents' beliefs and understandings, and parents affirmed teachers' beliefs and understandings. This point can be illustrated in an excerpt from a transcript. During the first conference, while the teacher was sharing work samples from the classroom, the parent commented on her daughter's writing progress, and the teacher affirmed the parent's observation:

PARENT: I have also seen that now in a month she already knows how to write her name by herself . . .

TEACHER: Yeah, at the beginning of the year there was the "G" here [*teacher displays her name starting from right to left*] and now, like today, she made it again like this here [*teacher displays the same sample*]. And then I said, "Oh Gina, you must start from that side, the 'G' here." And she did it herself later . . .

Later in the conference, as the parent presented her daughter's home portfolio, she shared an artifact from a visit the mother and child had made to the bank, and the teacher connected the artifact to the earlier conversation:

PARENT: So, I went to the bank. Then when I was in the front cashing a check, well, she [her daughter] made a transaction. [*Mother displays a withdrawal slip and mother and teacher both laugh.*]

TEACHER: Yeah! Her name is here, her name from left to right!

PARENT: So here, she took out one hundred dollars. [*They laugh.*]

Much later in the school year, during another conference, the conversation turned once again to the child's ability to write her name. The parent, again, related the teacher's evaluation to her own observations of her daughter in their daily interactions:

TEACHER: . . . She already writes—

PARENT: But now I see that . . . she writes her first name and last name by herself.

TEACHER: Yeah! Now we are working on this.

PARENT: And I already have a nice experience with her. We went to the bookstore to buy a book and then with the card that an adult has to sign. She told me, "No Mom, I am going to sign it myself." And she wrote her name—

TEACHER: Good.

PARENT: She told me, "No, Mom, I am going to sign it myself." And she wrote her name.

TEACHER: I am happy to hear that.

PARENT: Oh yes, she told me, "I know how to write my name. Mom, I am going to write it by myself."

TEACHER: Yeah, everyday we do that . . .

In her final interview, the teacher commented generally on how the mother related her own observations to those of the teacher: "So, I went first, and you know, she had a lot of comments as I was showing her [the child's] work, about, you know, what she was doing at home that was like that."

We reviewed a total of 34 conferences, and we were able to find episodes such as these in more than three-quarters of the conferences we reviewed. We concluded that, within these conferences, the portfolio served not only as a catalyst for conversations about home but also, importantly, as a way for parents and teacher to co-construct their understanding of the child as a literacy learner. The nature of the conversations as collaborative and supportive and, further, as different from previous parent–teacher conferences was evident in comments from many parents, but perhaps best articulated in this remark:

> He [her child] had gone with me the first time but she just gave him a book and she told us, you know, how he was and the level he was at. But now there was more conversation since I showed her all this. She noticed where he started, that he didn't know anything, and he progressed. He progressed a lot. It helped me because there was more communication with me talking to her and her having more to tell me about him. A conversation, because the other time, well, she showed me that this little paper and then I went. Not now, now we got deeper in the work that he is really doing, we were deeper, you know, in the conversation of knowing exactly his progress.

Parents were not alone in sensing the change in the nature of their conversations. Many teachers commented that the portfolio seemed to change the level of comfort in the conference. One teacher referred to a change in the balance of power, explaining, "Since she [the parent] had something to contribute, too, we came in on a more even level."

Second, the evidence suggested that sharing the portfolio led to increased or improved learning opportunities at home and at school. As parents described family literacy practices, teachers often offered suggestions for ways parents might further support their children's literacy development. In one example from the transcripts, the parent described to the teacher how she read with her child, and the teacher affirmed her actions:

> PARENT:　. . . when I read a book to her, right, she retains in her head what I have read to her. Later, I have turned the pages like this slowly, and she tells me what I have told her.
>
> TEACHER:　That is good. That is how she learns to read.

However, the teacher's feedback did not stop at affirmation. As the parent continued, the teacher helped the parent to acquire new strategies for guiding the child's response to literature:

> PARENT:　. . . I would always tell her, "[The child's name], what do you like most about the story?" And she told me "here" and I told her, "Why do you like that page here?" She told me because of the girl's scream. She liked it completely, she says that she is not afraid of monsters . . .
>
> TEACHER:　When you ask a question, things like why, you should ask more . . . she has to think or recall things about the story.

The conclusion that such exchanges had the potential to lead to ongoing parent–child learning interactions was supported by interview data. In a follow-up interview, the parent commented:

> I am going to continue . . . that is something that motivates me more . . . to continue providing my product, contributing with my ideas. And contributing here in the school. To continue working, right, with the school with the portfolio . . . because . . . I see that they value the work that one does, right? They value the work that one does.

The teacher also commented on the influence she thought the interactions during the conference had on parent–child interactions at home:

> During the first conference we had talked about [the fact that the child's] basic literacy skills were really good and her numeracy skills weren't so great, or they weren't at the same level as her literacy. So, I had mentioned that and I said, "Maybe that's something you [the mother] could work on because you obviously work on the literacy stuff." And, that was one of the areas where we saw a big change and I said that I'm sure it was from the work that she was doing with her at home.

Keeping and sharing a portfolio also seemed to encourage the parent to seek ways to collaborate with the teacher. During one interview, a teacher reported that when the parent brought her daughter to school each day, "At least once a week, she'll ask me, 'So, what are we doing this week?' So, I'll point things out that are going on around the room." The parent also commented on these interactions and provided explicit evidence of her follow-through: "This week, now, they are going to study the fish and the ocean in [the child's] classroom. Well, I have looked for books in the library that talk about fish and the ocean, right?"

We took the evidence to be an indication that with the home portfolio as a context for sharing family literacy events, three outcomes occurred: first, parents effectively and enthusiastically shared what they were doing; second, teachers affirmed the interactions and used them to inform parents about ways to continue to support their children's literacy learning; and third, by so doing, children's opportunities for literacy learning increased or improved.

Summary

Research in parent involvement teaches us that although virtually all parents are committed to supporting their children's academic success, there are differences in parents' perceptions about the types of actions they should take. Although mainstream teachers widely perceive parent involvement to include support for academic activities including reading and writing practice, many parents understand their role to be monitoring children's behavior and attendance, promoting respect for the teacher, and making certain that children are clean and well rested for school. When parents fail to attend school meetings, participate in field trips, or make particular inquiries about how to support academic activities, teachers draw the often erroneous conclusion that the parents "don't care" about their children's school experiences.

Further, although the evidence indicates that even with these differences in perceptions, parents with both low and high levels of education stand ready to support teachers in whatever requests they make, many teachers rarely ask anything of them. Rather, teachers sometimes act on an assumption that parents with limited English proficiency or limited formal education are unable to support their children's academic learning.

Studies indicate that effective parent involvement programs share some common characteristics: they are respectful of parents' knowledge, cultures, traditions, and personal circumstances; they seek reciprocity in learning between parents and teachers; they provide parents explicit instruction in the skills and strategies they expect them to use with their children; and they build the classroom curriculum at least partially on the children's family and community learning experiences.

At the ILP, these characteristics were woven into two particular parent involvement projects. The Parents as Classroom Storybook Readers Project built on parents' strengths as readers in both their first language and English, provided them an opportunity to spend time in classrooms and thereby advance their understanding of classroom literacy, and provided teachers a window on the many ways parents with low levels of formal education and limited English proficiency can support children's literacy learning. The Home-School Literacy Portfolio Project encouraged parents to document the many ways they and their children engage in family literacy by constructing a portfolio. It also encouraged parents to share the portfolio with their children's teacher during regularly scheduled parent–teacher conferences. Teachers were given the opportunity to explore and extend their understanding of family literacies and home–school partnerships by participating in a series of professional development seminars. The project led to beneficial conversations between parents and teachers about children's literacy learning both at home and at school and a deeper understanding among teachers of the ways parents and children share literacy at home, as well as to increased opportunities for children to learn in both settings.

The final chapter looks back over the entire ten-year Intergenerational Literacy Project effort—what we did, how we did it, and the outcomes we observed—with an eye toward going beyond it. What lessons does the ILP hold for work in supporting family literacy and developing home–school partnerships in general? What questions do we still have? What types of efforts might hold the answers to those questions?

NOTES

1. This project was funded through a three-year research grant from the U.S. Department of Education, National Institute of Early Childhood and Development, Award No. R307F60011.

CHAPTER

5

Learning and Thinking about Families, Schools, and Communities

The field of family literacy is a complex and muddy arena—one in which there is wide disagreement about the goals, purposes, and potential effects on the lives of those the programs are intended to serve. Some want family literacy interventions to "move families to self-sufficiency" (Darling, 1997, p. 3) by preparing parents for well-paying jobs; others reject this goal as ill founded and naïve, citing evidence that "the reading success equation has an insufficient proof for most Americans" (Edmondson & Shannon, 1998, p. 120). Some expect family literacy programs to "change the system of meaning within the home so children receive messages conveying the importance of education" (Darling & Hayes, 1988–89, p. 9), but others react to such a goal as unwarranted and disrespectful, citing research that is "unequivocal in concluding that almost all parents from all backgrounds care about the education of their children at school" (Swap, 1993, p. 25). The field is divided on how literacy and family literacy should be defined (Morrow, Paratore, Gaber, Harrison, & Tracey, 1993), on how interventions should be framed (Taylor, 1997), and on how program effects should be measured (Murphy, 1997; Johnston 1997).

In our own work, we attempted to quiet the noise in family literacy by situating our work in a theoretically grounded definition of literacy, in a research-based perspective on how linguistically and culturally different families use literacy in the conduct of their daily lives, and in research-based principles on how to teach and assess literacy. In this chapter, I return to each of the elements that framed the ILP—the definition of literacy, our understandings of the literate lives of linguistically and culturally different families, and effective teaching and testing practices— and revisit them, this time against the backdrop of ten years of project implementation. In doing so, I reflect on what we have learned about adult and family literacies, about family literacy programs, about children and school literacies, and about home–school partnerships.

Learning about Adult and Family Literacies

I begin this section with a simple thought: words matter. The ways we use words to describe and label individuals and the circumstances in their lives matter. In the Workforce Investment Partnership Act of 1998, commonly known as the Adult Education and Family Literacy Act, the U.S. Congress defined *literacy* as "an individual's ability to read, write, and speak in English, compute and solve problems, at levels of proficiency necessary to function on the job, in the family of the individual, and in society." When this definition of literacy was approved by Congress and signed into law by the President, it essentially labeled thousands of Americans as illiterate persons, whatever their levels of literacy proficiency in languages other than English. Yet, the work of the adults who have participated in the ILP defies the label of illiterate. Consider Gladis's story, composed first in Spanish, and with assistance in English:

> I write these few letters to express the two biggest presents God has given me, which are my two children. Little stars that came down from the sky to share their lives with me, presents that God has given me, so that I can educate them, teach them, and give them my greatest mother's love.
>
> I ask that God gives me love so that I can give it to those two. Ana is the name of my daughter, a name I gave her because it is the name of a servant of God who wanted a child and she could not have children, but God gave her one. And she had a son and named him Samuel and my son has Samuel as his second name because I asked God for a son and He gave him to me.
>
> For this reason, I write this short piece of history of the names of my two small children, stars that God Almighty has given me. (Intergenerational Literacy Project, 1996, p. 109)

Because Gladis was not able to compose this piece in English, she would not be counted as a literate person under the definition approved by the U.S. Congress. Yet, Gladis clearly has acquired "ways of thinking, cognitive abilities, facility in logic, abstraction and higher order mental operations . . . all integrally related to the achievement of literacy" (Street, 1995, p. 21). Should the fact that she has acquired these cognitive and intellectual functions in a language other than English cause us to deny her literacy?

Angelica, the author of the next piece, which was composed in Spanish and translated into English by a tutor, would also fail to meet the U.S. Congress's definition of a literate person:

> The differences between my country, El Salvador, and the United States with respect to school are in the ways teachers treat students and the kind of education students get. In the schools in my country, teachers arrange meetings with parents, and parents talk to their children and spend more time with them at home.
>
> In El Salvador, economically speaking, it is not good because parents have to buy all school supplies and uniforms. This was during the time I was attending school. Now, I think that everything has changed and there is more economic help for students.

When my parents and my uncles went to school, the lessons taught in first and second grade were so advanced that they were like what is taught in sixth grade today. Years ago in my country, teachers and parents were very strict with children's education and discipline. Teachers punished students very sternly. Sometimes, they hit them with a ruler made of bamboo and they put them in the corner of the classroom with their arms up. Parents also punished their children very sternly with wet ropes or belts. For example, my mother told me that their parents used to make them kneel on rice and maize.

On the contrary, in the United States, everything is different. There are many opportunities for our children to be able to study a lot so they can get a good job. Parents also have to work very hard. Sometimes, they have one or two jobs in order to support their children. The bad things are that there is not much communication between them and their children because parents work a lot and they get so tired from work that they just want to sleep. Sometimes when they come home from work, their children are already sleeping.

Another important thing for our children in this country is that they have libraries and computers to do their homework. This is good and also the teachers treat the students well.

I think that these differences have a positive impact on my children. My children make me very happy because they behave well at school and at home. I don't have problems with them. For example, my son Wilber is intelligent, he gets good grades, he is on the honor roll at his school and he wants to go to university. He has been accepted by the University of Massachusetts in Amherst, but he is still waiting to hear from other universities. He is worried because other universities have accepted four other classmates, but they haven't called him. He is also waiting for scholarships, but that comes after he has been accepted.

The whole family and I are very happy and proud because Wilber has had the opportunity to go to university. I thank God for having these wonderful and intelligent children. I also thank the teachers for teaching them and opening the path to a good life. (Intergenerational Literacy Project, 1999, p. 56)

Again the label doesn't fit—and, as we meet and talk with learners and browse through their portfolios, again and again we find evidence that contradicts the nationally sanctioned definition of literacy. Our understanding of what adults in the ILP know and are able to do has caused us to reject language that would have us characterize the adults with whom we work as illiterate. Our observations of the ways adults in the ILP use literacy in the course of their daily lives are consistent with and effectively characterized by Moll's (1992) description of the literate lives of the immigrant families he studied. He explained that the families he observed employed both formal and informal strategies to learn new skills. Formal strategies are those acquired through some sort of academic institution—schools, training programs, or workshops. Informal strategies are those that mobilize community and social resources—knowledge acquired through routine experiences. According to Moll, although literacy may mediate these strategies in different ways, it is virtually never absent:

> Formal strategies commonly depend heavily on literacy because institutional settings are frequently divorced from contexts where knowledge may be applied. Informal strategies, in contrast, tend to depend more on oral communications and observations, as well as on trial and error. This is not to say that literacy is absent or unimportant; rather that literacy plays a supplementary role, that is, it is used to build on and extend existing funds of knowledge . . . literacy is an unavoidable part of life in the social and economic context in which these households function. (p. 223)

Resisting the characterization of family literacy program participants as illiterate is not an academic endeavor; it is, instead, a pedagogical one. As noted by Scribner (1986), "The enterprise of defining literacy . . . becomes one of assessing what counts as literacy in the modern epoch in some given social context" (p. 9). The ways we perceive and describe those we teach has a fundamental influence on what and how we teach—on what we choose to count and value. When we acknowledge at the outset that participants enter a family literacy project with broad and deep funds of knowledge (Moll, Amanti, Neff, & Gonzalez, 1992), and we validate what they know by using their family and community experiences and their home languages as the foundation for teaching and learning, we change the context of the learning community. We begin to build the shared cultural and social norms that are known to influence the educational success of learners outside the mainstream of American society (Foster, 1993). By so doing, we tell something of ourselves and our values, and as Gundlach (1992) noted, we engage in an intellectual endeavor that is likely to take us beyond the teaching of reading and writing:

> Sometimes unwillingly, sometimes unwittingly, we who teach regularly teach something of the values of the place in which we teach, along with whatever we teach about the roles and conventions and possibilities of reading and writing. If becoming literate always involves more than being taught, teaching reading and writing always involves more than teaching reading and writing. (Gundlach, 1992, p.367)

And so, I return again to the words that I used to begin this discussion of the literate lives of the families we have taught over the first ten years of the ILP: words matter. To describe these adults as illiterate is wrong. They tell us on intake and they show us throughout their course of study that they use language, orally and in print, each and every day to mediate their family, community, and work routines. What most of them lack is proficiency in English and familiarity with the ways literacy is used to negotiate life in U.S. society. They are not illiterate but rather, as Purcell-Gates (1995) suggested, differently literate.

Learning about Family Literacy Programs

The high attendance and retention rates achieved by ILP parents suggest that the program offers learning experiences that adults perceive to be worthy of their time and effort. In addition, writing samples indicate small but steady gains across all learners, and parents report increased uses of literacy alone and with their children. A recent essay by Edmondson and Shannon (1998) on literacy for the twenty-first century is helpful in understanding the programmatic features that account for these positive results. In their article, Edmondson and Shannon (1998) challenged educators to "retheorize literacy to help all citizens participate in public life" (p. 120). They explained that:

> we need literacy education that will help all citizens to develop their faculties of communication, deliberation, and judgment. We should take these steps not to make them rich but to allow all to participate fully in the civic life of their communities and their relationships to larger political and cultural bodies. (p. 120)

The need that Edmondson and Shannon articulated is evident in the experiences of many of our learners, and it is exemplified in a narrative written by one of the parents, Francilia:

> For eight years I had a problem with rats. I moved from Boston to Chelsea to rent an apartment. Days passed by and I started to see rats in my apartment. At that time, I was pregnant with my daughter Jennifer. I went to the hospital and when I came back home, more days passed by and more rats were coming. One night, there was a rat in my daughter's crib. I called my sister and I moved to her house for a few days.
>
> Later, I talked with the landlord, but I had a problem with him because he said that I did not speak English and that I had not communicated with him. We went to court, but the judge did not agree with the landlord. He had to give me my money back and I had to move to a new apartment with my two children.
>
> Since that time, good things and bad things have happened to me and my family. People who come to this country have to live with the law and improve themselves to be able to continue living in this country. I have been in this country and I think it is like a jungle in which one must learn to survive. That's why I decided to learn English in order to improve myself, to get a better job, and to support my children with their education. I also want to learn English because it is important to speak more than one language in this country.
>
> It took me so long to come to school, but it is never too late to learn. (Intergenerational Literacy Project, 1999, p. 99)

We have tried to meet the needs of such parents by implementing what Auerbach (1997) called a social change perspective. Building on the work of Freire (1970) in critical literacy, Auerbach described this approach to literacy instruction as one that combines a multiple-literacies perspective—which builds on "the culture-specific literacy practices and ways of knowing" (p. 651) that learners bring with them—with an emphasis on empowering learners to change the "conditions which cause marginalization" (p. 655) in their lives. In the social change perspective,

> Change is seen to come about through a gradual process of struggling with inequities wherever they occur; the struggles in the more immediate domains (family, classroom) are both a part of and a rehearsal for struggles in the broader domains; the broader changes come about not just through individual effort but through collective action. Personal empowerment, thus, cannot be separated from social change: empowerment is defined not in individual terms (i.e., in terms of gaining self-esteem and taking control of one's life), but in social terms (in terms of challenging the institutional forces that impede access). (Auerbach, 1997, p. 655)

Parents in the ILP have not taken on social change as a public cause; that is, we have not organized or assisted parents in organizing rallies or marches on the State House. Rather, parents have chosen to focus on causes that have a daily impact on them or their children. They persistently want to examine and discuss issues related to employment and request practice in filling out forms, interviewing, understanding how to prepare for new areas of work, and identifying new companies. They rely enormously on the social networks that develop within the literacy classes, particularly to learn about job openings and employment opportunities. Health care also represents an issue of high interest. Although nearly all of the children have health insurance, many of the parents do not. Often, the reason is lack of information about how to make their way through the health care system. We provide information that will help them do so. Another area of interest is home buying. Despite the many programs available for low-income families in this community, many parents are unaware that home ownership is an option for them. We provide information that helps them understand the opportunities available to them. Perhaps the most frequent issue raised by parents is that of understanding the complexities of secondary and postsecondary education. They are faced with many choices as parents of secondary students, among them placement in special education, bilingual education, alternative education, college preparatory, or vocational programs. These are often the focus of class readings and discussions. In considering the social change issues that have dominated ILP classes, the project director offered the following comment in an e-mail correspondence:

> Social issues in the classroom nearly always arise from learners' interests. No, that's not true. Social issues addressed in the classroom are only successfully built on when they arise from learners' interests. When we try to push our agenda on parents and they don't see the relevance of what we consider to be major issues, they turn off. One hot topic that has been introduced by teachers and has been met with disinterest is domestic violence—sometimes. On a couple of occasions, the same topic has been brought up by a learner, in conversation with a teacher or tutor or in writing. When lessons focused on the issue then, it led to rich discussion and thoughtful writing.

Not all of the ILP curriculum is focused on social change. An anecdote Degener (1998) reported illustrates a lesson that was intended to build on the multiple literacies that learners bring to class, independent of a particular social purpose. Degener set out to describe what a "critical literacy approach to family literacy look[s] like in practice" (p. 1). In the conduct of that study, she visited one of the project's classes 12 times and collected 20 hours of data. In her final report, she provided the following description of a lesson she observed:

> The class read the Serbo-Croatian poem, "The King of Magla and Vlaga." . . . To begin with, the Bosnian students present in class that day, Sabina and Svenka, were obviously delighted to see a familiar story in class. Gabriela and Tereza asked them to translate the Croatian words . . . into English, which they gladly did. In fact, Sabina made a point of getting everybody to pronounce the words correctly. It was clear from the smile on her face, and her imposing stature as she stood to be heard, that she took a lot of pride in this role as an expert. It must be noted, too, that Sabina had been having a very hard time lately, financially and emotionally, and had been very glum and withdrawn in class. On this day in particular, she had come into class with her shoulders hunched, her head hanging down, and had sat at a table quietly, without talking to anyone else. For her to be standing up only half an hour later and loudly leading the class in the pronunciation of Croatian words was a remarkable turnaround for her. Tereza and Gabriela allowed Sabina and Svenka to continue on in their expert roles by asking them to work with separate groups as they read the poem and attempted to summarize its meaning. Understanding the poem proved difficult for the Latino/a students, as it was a story they were unfamiliar with, and the figurative language of the poem proved to be quite difficult to translate into Spanish. . . . The teachers picked up on the fact that students were having some difficulty understanding the meaning of the poem, so they decided on the spot that students should act out the poem. The students readily agreed, and what followed were many hilarious moments, as different students acted out the poem two times. (p. x)

Degener commented on the learners' actions and reactions to this text:

> I was really impressed by Claudia's willingness to narrate the story, because she is not at all confident about her English, and generally says very little in class. Asking the students to act out the poem was a great instructional decision, because it gave the students the opportunity to visualize what the poem was saying and to see what the figurative language actually meant. Everybody had the opportunity to make suggestions to the actors, and this showed that they were beginning to understand what the poem meant. Equally important was how well the class worked together on this task. . . . After class, students were still giggling and talking together as they walked over to the child care room to pick up their children. (p. 24)

Of course, texts of this type do not help learners to address issues of social change in their lives. They do, however, create a context for building intercultural awareness and understanding. In addition, they provide both a foundation and a context in which learners can use existing literacies as they work to acquire new literacies. It is also important to note that the literacy lesson that grew out of this particular text was shaped not only by the cultural relevance of the text to some learners but also by the cultural and linguistic diversity of the classroom. In a context characterized by cultural and linguistic homogeneity, it is likely that the lesson that developed would have differed substantially.

In sum, as we try to understand the factors that contributed to the positive outcomes ILP learners achieved, it seems likely that a combination of factors explain the results. First, taking both a multiple literacies and a social change approach to learning expanded the types of text and the general curriculum available for instruction. Of importance was the single criterion of *relevance*—the texts that learners heard, read, and discussed were worthy of their attention, either because they were culturally relevant and, as such, built on available funds of knowledge (Moll & Greenberg, 1992) or because they were socially relevant and, therefore, were helpful in accomplishing personal, family, or community goals. In addition, the emphasis on both personal and family goals seemed to be important. Parents clearly were motivated by their desire to help their children succeed, but they were also motivated by their personal goals and ambitions.

Second, as suggested by Moll (1998) and Vasquez, Pease-Alverez, and Shannon (1994), the bilingual, bicultural, and biliterate approach to instruction expanded learners' resources for learning. Although printed text was available in English only, the opportunity for learners to use their first language to prepare for reading enhanced their foundation for understanding. Similarly, the opportunity to respond to text in the first language enabled learners to display their understanding and interpretation of text written in English before they had acquired requisite oral proficiency in English, and the opportunity to respond first in the native language provided the foundation for response in English.

Third, forming groups of multilingual, multicultural learners created opportunities for learners to display their individual literacies and their personal histories. In addition, however, multilingual, multicultural classrooms were demanding on teachers. The staffing plan the ILP utilized, which includes two teachers and three tutors to each class of 25 parents, allowed flexible use of homogeneous and heterogeneous grouping options to meet individual needs. Further, the context of homogeneous and heterogeneous small-group discussions and the use of the pedagogical strategy of the instructional conversation (Tharp & Gallimore, 1988; Goldenberg, 1992/1993) provided parents with both the opportunity and the support to engage in discourse that extended both their language and literacy knowledge.

Fourth, the ILP differs from many family literacy program models (in particular, the Even Start and National Center for Family Literacy models) in its emphasis on influencing the practice of family literacy by teaching the parent about shared literacy practices that they might embed within the fabric of daily family routines, rather than on bringing the parent and child together outside the home to engage in shared literacy activities, or PACT time (Logan, 1999). Our rationale for this particular program characteristic was based on two factors: we believe that parents are capable of understanding and implementing particular shared literacy practices following explanation and discussion, without the benefit of a demonstration and practice with their own child under the watchful eye of a teacher; moreover, because many ILP parents who participate in the ILP have both preschool and schoolage children, and because parents attend ILP classes while their children are in school, bringing parents and children together during the conduct of family literacy classes would necessitate pulling children out of their regular education activities. We rejected this option on the basis of evidence that the array of pull-out programs intended to support children with special learning needs actually result in a high degree of fragmentation and incoherence in their instructional programs (Johnston & Allington, 1991). Some programs choose to offer parent–child activities in the evening or on the weekends. Conversations with parents, teachers, and other service providers convinced us that parents who were attending literacy classes, working in or outside their homes, and tending to their routine parental and spousal responsibilities had little time for an additional class. We therefore chose to embed family literacy training activities within the context of the adult literacy classes. Parents' self-reported data collected on entry and exit from the project indicated increases in both daily and weekly shared literacy practices. Parents also told us in interviews and during classroom discussions that in those cases where particular shared literacy activities were already common activities, such as storybook reading, the ILP did not increase the frequency of the activity but did influence the nature of the interaction, as parents learned to prepare children for the types of literacy practices that would contribute to their success in early literacy. We take the combination of frequency and interview data as evidence that embedding family literacy training within the context of adult literacy classes is an effective practice. At the same time, however, we are mindful that there is no "right way" to support family literacy. Although the practice of embedding family literacy instruction is effective within this particular community, a range of other strategies, including parent and child activity time, may well prove beneficial in other contexts.

Learning about Children and School Literacies

In earlier work examining the school success of children whose parents participated in the Intergenerational Literacy Project (Paratore, Melzi, & Krol-Sinclair, 1999), my colleagues and I concluded:

> Contrary to commonly-held beliefs, we did not find that parents' proficiency in English, years of education, or personal literacy skills played an important role in their ability to support their children's academic success. We did not find parents who were not involved, not interested, or not dedicated to their children's learning. We also did not find instances of either success or failure that could be explained solely by the types of events that occurred either at home or at school. Instead, we came to understand that, for these children, success in school was a complex process, dependent both on the actions of parents and teachers separately, and perhaps most importantly, on their interactions. Children who succeeded had parents and teachers who took actions that were, either by design or by accident, both complementary and consistent. (p. 107)

As I now look back on ten years of project implementation and the additional data we have collected, I see no evidence that challenges our earlier conclusions.

Across the data, where children were successful in school, they had a high level of parental support and involvement in academic learning; that is, a parent read to or with them, helped with homework, monitored their performance in school by asking questions of them or of the teacher, and admonished them to be on time, to behave courteously, and to be respectful of the teacher. In addition, successful students also had effective and intensive instruction in literacy in school; that is, they had teachers who offered systematic and explicit instruction in reading and writing, and whose classrooms were orderly and print-rich.

In cases where children experienced serious difficulty in school, their failure was not explained by the role their parents played in their academic learning. Instead, there were complex and varied reasons for their failure and few similarities in their profiles. The array of factors included relatively weak or inconsistent school instruction, inconsistent home support, transience, divorce, low motivation, and, in one case, a possible learning disability. In every case where a child was failing, there was more than one obstacle to academic success.

Although the data related to correlates of school success and school failure are quite consistent, other evidence raises a question of a different type. In the relatively small sample of 23 children, we found that teachers reported high academic achievement and positive attitudes toward school and learning both on entry and on exit from the program. Although the sample is too small to allow generalization, if the finding holds up to larger and more randomized sampling, it might lead to several important questions. For example, although on one hand these data speak to the children's school success and are therefore very positive, on the other hand, one could legitimately ask if projects such as the ILP are actually recruiting and serving families who are *most* in need—families of children who would fail in school if their parents did not have the learning opportunity offered by intervention programs. Confirming data might also raise questions about what the goal of family literacy programs should be. Suppose expected effects of family literacy interventions were not higher test scores for children but rather greater collaboration among parents and teachers, greater interest and practice of reading and writing among children, or increased parent–child literacy interactions—not for the sake of increasing school achievement but for the purpose of improving family, school, and community relationships? Should the most important purpose be the improvement of children's test scores, or should we seek broader goals of family literacy interventions? If it is the former, it should change the ways we recruit and enroll families into programs. If it is the latter, it should change the ways we evaluate project outcomes and effectiveness.

Learning about Home–School Partnerships

A few days before I sat down to compose this final chapter, I chatted with a teacher as we waited together for the start of a meeting in an urban elementary school. When I asked her how long she had been teaching in this particular school, she replied that she had started there nearly 25 years earlier. "In those years," she said somewhat wistfully, "the mothers were lovely." As noted in earlier sections of this book, the belief that parental attitudes toward education have changed is quite common among teachers, administrators, and policy makers. Some may recall that in 1990, U.S. Secretary of Education Lauro Cavazos made headlines when he stated that Hispanic parents "deserved much of the blame for a high dropout rate among their children that could have dire consequences for the American economy" (Suro, 1990, p. B8). In 1998, the National Center for Education Statistics reported, "Given a list of concerns that might impede parent involvement in schools, the barrier named by the highest percentage of schools was lack of time on the part of parents" (p. 2). The root of these beliefs might be traced at least partially to insufficient attention to the full slate of existing data. For example, Sable and Stennett (1998) reported, "In 1996, Hispanic children, ages 3–5, were less likely to have been read to in the past week or to have visited a library in the past month than white children" (p. 2). It is, perhaps, easy to interpret such findings as evidence of parents' lack of concern about education or lack of time for their children. However, other evidence disputes this interpretation. Based on a recent study of parent involvement, The National Center for Education Statistics (1998) found that "parents of more that 80 percent of students reported attending a general meeting or a scheduled meeting with their children's teacher" (p. 3). Data from the same study led to a finding that "parents of black and Hispanic students were more likely than parents of white students to help their children with homework three or more times a week" (p. 4). These findings are consistent with evidence from numerous ethnographic studies of linguistically and culturally different families (Delgado-Gaitan, 1994, 1996; Heath, 1983; Taylor & Dorsey-Gaines, 1988; Valdés, 1996; Vasquez, Pease-Alvarez, & Shannon, 1996).

The apparent divide between what teachers believe about parents and what parents actually do is mirrored in the beliefs and practices of both teachers and parents documented in our investigations. At the outset of the home–school portfolio project, questionnaire data indicated that most teachers perceived parents as generally uninterested in their children's schooling and as unable to support their learning, largely because of language differences. Teachers believed that their impressions were supported by parents' failure to attend general meetings and by their inability to communicate with them in English. Questionnaire data from parents, however, provided substantially different findings. Parents believed that they were responsible to monitor both behavior and academic performance, and they reported that they did so. Although teachers were correct in their observation that some parents rarely attended school meetings, they were incorrect in using this information as a measure of parent involvement in their children's learning. Parental actions included both helping children with homework assigned by teachers and initiating their own assignments when the children had none. In addition, evidence indicated that parents often assumed responsibility for teaching children to read and write in their native language.

Of importance, however, is the influence that special projects had on teachers' perceptions. By the end of both the Home–School Portfolio project and the Parents as Classroom Storybook Readers Project, many teachers perceived parents through different eyes and particularly recognized that many of the children's parents had both the motivation and the ability to support their children academically. We also learned that, although teachers were persistent in their view that the bridge to home–school partnerships was one-way—from school to home—they also were enthusiastic in their desire to explore the types of strategies that they could implement to collaborate more effectively with parents. We found that teachers wanted to establish collaboration but found it difficult to do so. When given the opportunity to learn about strategies to establish home–school partnerships, many teachers were eager to participate.

We also learned about the potential for special projects to influence parental actions. We found that particular training programs did not necessarily introduce new practices to parents; that is, most of the parents reported on entry to the project that they engaged in storybook reading, storytelling, and homework help at least occasionally. But special training projects did help parents change the ways they shared literacy with children. For example, parents reported greater frequency of storybook reading and increased conversation and verbal interaction during book sharing. We also found that special projects could help parents acquire a greater understanding of schools and classrooms. As noted in Chapter 4, parents who participated in the classroom as storybook readers expressed fuller understanding of the ways children learn to read and write in classrooms and of what is expected of children. Such experiences are especially important for parents who have been educated outside the United States and lack familiarity with practices common in U.S. classrooms.

In sum, our experiences and our evidence lead us to conclude that special practices and programs can enhance parents' understanding of the classroom and classroom literacies and, as well, can expand teachers' understanding of families and family literacies. The evidence led us back to Epstein's (1986) conclusion that if we as teachers believe that parent involvement is critical for children's success in school, then we must accept our responsibility to take actions that will help parents to fulfill their roles. As Serpell (1997) noted, assuming this responsibility and carrying out effective actions is likely to require a "quite different type of social interaction . . . one that involves the negotiation of a shared understanding" (p. 595) between parents and teachers.

Looking Back and Looking Forward

The decade of work in the Intergenerational Literacy Project has taught us some important lessons. We have learned, for example, that ethnicity, language, years of education, and socioeconomic status tell us little about the ways parents use literacy to achieve their personal goals, about their interest in their children's educational experience, or about their ability to support their children academically. We have also learned that despite the predictive value of the same constellation of factors for children's success in school, they tell us little about individual children's chances of success; many children of ILP parents who are poor or linguistically and culturally different enter and exit the project as successful students. We have learned of the enormous power of teachers to make a difference in the lives of both parents and children; teachers can effectively open or close doors that provide entry to learning. Finally, we have learned that projects such as the ILP can make a difference as they help parents to co-construct meaning with other adults, with their children, and with their children's teachers.

At the same time, we are mindful of risks inherent in home–school partnership initiatives. Lareau (1994) cautioned that "although family–school partnerships are overwhelmingly defined as helpful for children, there is clear evidence that parents' actions can have unintended, negative consequences" (p. 67). We, too, have seen such evidence: teachers who interpreted parents' inquiries and attempts to learn about the classroom curriculum as "pushy"; parents who proudly shared family portfolios that were filled with school-like worksheets and practice activities; teachers who were resentful of the imposition of parent involvement initiatives on their time. Although such consequences clearly concern us, we see them not as reason to turn away from family literacy and home–school partnership intervention initiatives but rather as reason to heighten our awareness of the need to develop programs around the principle of negotiated and collaborative interactions. Shockley, Michalove, and Allen (1995) reminded us that to effectively engage parents and teachers in a joint effort, they did not try to "impose our vision of literacy but to develop relationships with families where we could learn about what already existed in the families and connect that with the literacy classroom community" (p. 94). When collaboration grows out of mutual respect and understanding, there is greater likelihood that the ongoing discourse will be honest and responsive to the needs of all participants. As such, I believe it holds the potential to open doors, open minds, and open opportunities for learning for parents, teachers, and children.

APPENDIX A
Learner Intake Interview

Intergenerational Literacy Project
Learner interview

Data entry date [   ]

First name [   ]   Last name [   ]

Address [   ]   Telephone [   ]

Current status [   ]

Entry date [   ]   Class [   ]

Intake date [   ]   Relationship [   ]

Exit date [   ]   Country of origin [   ]

Commitment [   ]

Cycles awarded/attendance [   ]   Notes [   ]

Children

First	Last	Gender	DOB	School	Grade	Teacher	Bring to ILP

Language of interview [   ]   Interviewer [   ]

Gender: ○ M ○ F

Ethnicity:
○ Latino/Latina   ○ White, not Hispanic
○ Asian/Pacific Islander   ○ Native American/Alaskan native
○ Black, not Hispanic   ○ Other…

Age:
○ 16-24
○ 25-44
○ 45-59
○ 60+

Length of time in U.S. [   ]   Length of time in Chelsea [   ]

Employment status:
○ Employed full-time   ○ Unemployed and not seeking work   ○ Retired
○ Employed part-time   ○ Currently laid off
○ Unemployed and seeking work   ○ Homemaker

Where do you work? [   ]   Length of time in current job [   ]

What do you do? [   ]

Previous employment [   ]   What did you do? [   ]

Do you receive public assistance? ○ Yes ○ No   What type? [   ]

Intergenerational Literacy Project

Learner interview

Data entry date [   ]

Years of formal schooling in another country		Years of formal schooling in U.S.		High school diploma or equivalent?
○ 0 ○ 8		○ 0 ○ 8		○ Diploma
○ 1 ○ 9		○ 1 ○ 9		○ GED in Eng.
○ 2 ○ 10		○ 2 ○ 10		○ GED in L1
○ 3 ○ 11		○ 3 ○ 11		○ none
○ 4 ○ 12		○ 4 ○ 12		
○ 5 ○ 13+		○ 5 ○ 13+		
○ 6 ○ Other…		○ 6 ○ Other…		
○ 7		○ 7		

Where studied? [   ]

Prior ESOL [○ Yes ○ No]   Prior ABE [○ Yes ○ No] Where studied? [   ]

First language [   ]   Other language(s) [   ]

English proficiency (self-assessment)
○ I speak no English.
○ I know a few important words, but I speak very little English.
○ I know enough English to carry on some conversations.
○ I speak English confidently.

Comments [   ]

In which language(s) do you read? [   ]

In which language(s) do you write? [   ]

How did you hear about this program? [   ]

What are your reasons for enrolling in this program? (Check all that apply.)

☐ to improve spoken English
☐ to improve reading competence
☐ to improve writing competence
☐ to improve math skills
☐ to learn about computers
☐ to handle everyday tasks (e.g., talking to physicians, paying bills, making appointments)
☐ to prepare for future employment
☐ to earn a high school diploma
☐ to support my children's learning
☐ Other…

What else would you like to learn? [   ]

Intergenerational Literacy Project

Learner interview

Data entry date [   ]

Before entering the program, how often did you read outside of class during a typical week?

adult books? ○ daily ○ 2-3x weekly ○ once a week ○ 2x/month ○ rarely ○ never ○ N/A ○ Yes ○ No
language(s) [   ]   specifics [   ]

newspapers? ○ daily ○ 2-3x weekly ○ once a week ○ 2x/month ○ rarely ○ never ○ N/A ○ Yes ○ No
language(s) [   ]   specifics [   ]

magazines? ○ daily ○ 2-3x weekly ○ once a week ○ 2x/month ○ rarely ○ never ○ N/A ○ Yes ○ No
language(s) [   ]   specifics [   ]

mail? ○ daily ○ 2-3x weekly ○ once a week ○ 2x/month ○ rarely ○ never ○ N/A ○ Yes ○ No
language(s) [   ]   specifics [   ]

forms or applications?
○ daily ○ 2-3x weekly ○ once a week ○ 2x/month ○ rarely ○ never ○ N/A ○ Yes ○ No
language(s) [   ]   specifics [   ]

Bible or other religious materials?
○ daily ○ 2-3x weekly ○ once a week ○ 2x/month ○ rarely ○ never ○ N/A ○ Yes ○ No
language(s) [   ]   specifics [   ]

information for my job?
○ daily ○ 2-3x weekly ○ once a week ○ 2x/month ○ rarely ○ never ○ N/A ○ Yes ○ No
language(s) [   ]   specifics [   ]

school information?
○ daily ○ 2-3x weekly ○ once a week ○ 2x/month ○ rarely ○ never ○ N/A ○ Yes ○ No
language(s) [   ]   specifics [   ]

other? [   ]   language(s) [   ]
how often? ○ daily ○ 2-3x weekly ○ once a week ○ 2x/month ○ rarely ○ never ○ N/A ○ Yes ○ No

Is there anything else you would like to read? [   ]
What do you do if you come to a word you can't read? [   ]
If you don't understand what you read, what do you do? [   ]
What do you do to help you remember what you read? [   ]
What are the characteristics of a good reader? [   ]

Intergenerational Literacy Project

Learner interview

Data entry date [   ]

Before entering the program, how often did you write outside of class during a typical week?

letters? ○ daily ○ 2-3x weekly ○ once a week ○ 2x/month ○ rarely ○ never ○ N/A ○ Yes ○ No

    language(s) [   ]   specifics [   ]

notes? ○ daily ○ 2-3x weekly ○ once a week ○ 2x/month ○ rarely ○ never ○ N/A ○ Yes ○ No

    language(s) [   ]   specifics [   ]

checks and bills? ○ daily ○ 2-3x weekly ○ once a week ○ 2x/month ○ rarely ○ never ○ N/A ○ Yes ○ No

    language(s) [   ]   specifics [   ]

forms and applications?

    ○ daily ○ 2-3x weekly ○ once a week ○ 2x/month ○ rarely ○ never ○ N/A ○ Yes ○ No

    language(s) [   ]   specifics [   ]

shopping lists? ○ daily ○ 2-3x weekly ○ once a week ○ 2x/month ○ rarely ○ never ○ N/A ○ Yes ○ No

    language(s) [   ]   specifics [   ]

journal/diary? ○ daily ○ 2-3x weekly ○ once a week ○ 2x/month ○ rarely ○ never ○ N/A ○ Yes ○ No

    language(s) [   ]   specifics [   ]

appointments on calendar?

    ○ daily ○ 2-3x weekly ○ once a week ○ 2x/month ○ rarely ○ never ○ N/A ○ Yes ○ No

    language(s) [   ]   specifics [   ]

homework? ○ daily ○ 2-3x weekly ○ once a week ○ 2x/month ○ rarely ○ never ○ N/A ○ Yes ○ No

    language(s) [   ]   specifics [   ]

work-related writing?

    ○ daily ○ 2-3x weekly ○ once a week ○ 2x/month ○ rarely ○ never ○ N/A ○ Yes ○ No

    language(s) [   ]   specifics [   ]

stories or poems? ○ daily ○ 2-3x weekly ○ once a week ○ 2x/month ○ rarely ○ never ○ N/A ○ Yes ○ No

    language(s) [   ]   specifics [   ]

other? [   ]   language(s) [   ]

    how often? ○ daily ○ 2-3 times weekly ○ once a week ○ 2x/month ○ rarely ○ never ○ N/A

Is there anything else you would like to write? [   ]

What do you do if you can't spell a word? [   ]

What do you do to check your writing? [   ]

How do you know when something you've written is good? [   ]

Intergenerational Literacy Project

Learner interview

Data entry date [   ]

Shared Literacy

Before you enrolled in the program, how often did you:

go to the library with your child(ren)?

○ daily ○ 2-3 times weekly ○ once a week ○ 2x/month ○ rarely ○ never ○ N/A

Comments [   ]

buy books? ○ daily ○ 2-3 times weekly ○ once a week ○ 2x/month ○ rarely ○ never ○ N/A

Comments [   ]

read stories with your child(ren)?

○ daily ○ 2-3 times weekly ○ once a week ○ 2x/month ○ rarely ○ never ○ N/A

Comments [   ]

tell stories to your child(ren)?

○ daily ○ 2-3 times weekly ○ once a week ○ 2x/month ○ rarely ○ never ○ N/A

Comments [   ]

ask about your child(ren)'s homework?

○ daily ○ 2-3 times weekly ○ once a week ○ 2x/month ○ rarely ○ never ○ N/A

Comments [   ]

help with your child(ren)'s homework?

○ daily ○ 2-3 times weekly ○ once a week ○ 2x/month ○ rarely ○ never ○ N/A

Comments [   ]

write notes/messages to your child(ren)?

○ daily ○ 2-3 times weekly ○ once a week ○ 2x/month ○ rarely ○ never ○ N/A

Comments [   ]

Approximately how many books do you have? [   ]

Approximately how many books do your children have? [   ]

Comments [   ]

In what ways do you and your family participate in your local community?

[   ]

Intergenerational Literacy Project

Learner interview

Data entry date [   ]

CHILDREN'S SCHOOL PERFORMANCE

Child #1   Child's name [   ]   Grade [   ]

How would you describe your child's attitude toward school?

○ My child almost always likes to go to school.
○ My child's attitude about school changes often. Some days s/he likes it and some days s/he doesn't.
○ My child does not like school.
○ I'm not sure about my child's attitude toward school.

How does your child do in school?

○ My child always receives good grades and good reports from school.
○ My child usually receives good grades and good reports from school.
○ My child sometimes receives good grades/reports and sometimes receives poor grades/ reports from school.
○ My child usually receives poor grades and poor reports from school.
○ I am not sure how my child does in school.

How often do you communicate with your child(ren)'s teacher?

○ daily
○ once a week
○ monthly
○ a few times a year
○ never
○ (2-3 times/week)
○ (2x/month)
○ (rarely)

In what ways do you communicate with your child's teacher?

☐ notes or letters
☐ telephone calls
☐ conferences
☐ conversations when I bring my child to or pick my child up from school

For what reasons do you contact your child's teacher?

Comments

APPENDIX B

Learner Exit Interview

Intergenerational Literacy Project

Learner Exit Form

Data entry date [   ]

First name [   ]   Last name [   ]

Language of interview [   ]   Interviewer [   ]

English proficiency
(self-assessment)
- ○ I speak no English.
- ○ I know a few important words, but I speak very little English.
- ○ I know enough English to carry on some conversations.
- ○ I speak English confidently.

Comments [   ]

In which language(s) do you read? [   ]

In which language(s) do you write? [   ]

Intergenerational Literacy Project

Learner Exit Form

Data entry date [   ]

How often do you read outside of class during a typical week?

adult books? ○ daily ○ 2-3x weekly ○ once a week ○ 2x/month ○ rarely ○ never ○ N/A ○ Yes ○ No
language(s) [   ]   specifics [   ]

newspapers? ○ daily ○ 2-3x weekly ○ once a week ○ 2x/month ○ rarely ○ never ○ N/A ○ Yes ○ No
language(s) [   ]   specifics [   ]

magazines? ○ daily ○ 2-3x weekly ○ once a week ○ 2x/month ○ rarely ○ never ○ N/A ○ Yes ○ No
language(s) [   ]   specifics [   ]

mail? ○ daily ○ 2-3x weekly ○ once a week ○ 2x/month ○ rarely ○ never ○ N/A ○ Yes ○ No
language(s) [   ]   specifics [   ]

forms or applications?
○ daily ○ 2-3x weekly ○ once a week ○ 2x/month ○ rarely ○ never ○ N/A ○ Yes ○ No
language(s) [   ]   specifics [   ]

Bible or other religious materials?
○ daily ○ 2-3x weekly ○ once a week ○ 2x/month ○ rarely ○ never ○ N/A ○ Yes ○ No
language(s) [   ]   specifics [   ]

information for my job?
○ daily ○ 2-3x weekly ○ once a week ○ 2x/month ○ rarely ○ never ○ N/A ○ Yes ○ No
language(s) [   ]   specifics [   ]

school information?
○ daily ○ 2-3x weekly ○ once a week ○ 2x/month ○ rarely ○ never ○ N/A ○ Yes ○ No
language(s) [   ]   specifics [   ]

other? [   ]   language(s) [   ]
how often? ○ daily ○ 2-3x weekly ○ once a week ○ 2x/month ○ rarely ○ never ○ N/A ○ Yes ○ No

Is there anything else you would like to read? [   ]
What do you do if you come to a word you can't read? [   ]

If you don't understand what you read, what do you do? [   ]
What do you do to help you remember what you read? [   ]
What are the characteristics of a good reader? [   ]

Intergenerational Literacy Project

Learner Exit Form

Data entry date [   ]

How often do you write outside of class during a typical week?

letters? ○ daily ○ 2-3x weekly ○ once a week ○ 2x/month ○ rarely ○ never ○ N/A ○ Yes ○ No

language(s) [   ] specifics [   ]

notes? ○ daily ○ 2-3x weekly ○ once a week ○ 2x/month ○ rarely ○ never ○ N/A ○ Yes ○ No

language(s) [   ] specifics [   ]

checks and bills? ○ daily ○ 2-3x weekly ○ once a week ○ 2x/month ○ rarely ○ never ○ N/A ○ Yes ○ No

language(s) [   ] specifics [   ]

forms and applications?

○ daily ○ 2-3x weekly ○ once a week ○ 2x/month ○ rarely ○ never ○ N/A ○ Yes ○ No

language(s) [   ] specifics [   ]

shopping lists? ○ daily ○ 2-3x weekly ○ once a week ○ 2x/month ○ rarely ○ never ○ N/A ○ Yes ○ No

language(s) [   ] specifics [   ]

journal/diary? ○ daily ○ 2-3x weekly ○ once a week ○ 2x/month ○ rarely ○ never ○ N/A ○ Yes ○ No

language(s) [   ] specifics [   ]

appointments on calendar?

○ daily ○ 2-3x weekly ○ once a week ○ 2x/month ○ rarely ○ never ○ N/A ○ Yes ○ No

language(s) [   ] specifics [   ]

homework? ○ daily ○ 2-3x weekly ○ once a week ○ 2x/month ○ rarely ○ never ○ N/A ○ Yes ○ No

language(s) [   ] specifics [   ]

work-related writing?

○ daily ○ 2-3x weekly ○ once a week ○ 2x/month ○ rarely ○ never ○ N/A ○ Yes ○ No

language(s) [   ] specifics [   ]

stories or poems? ○ daily ○ 2-3x weekly ○ once a week ○ 2x/month ○ rarely ○ never ○ N/A ○ Yes ○ No

language(s) [   ] specifics [   ]

other? [   ] language(s) [   ]

how often? ○ daily ○ 2-3 times weekly ○ once a week ○ 2x/month ○ rarely ○ never ○ N/A

Is there anything else you would like to write? [   ]

What do you do if you can't spell a word? [   ]

What do you do to check your writing? [   ]

How do you know when something you've written is good? [   ]

Intergenerational Literacy Project

Learner Exit Form

Data entry date [   ]

Shared Literacy

How often do you:

go to the library with your child(ren)?

○ daily ○ 2-3 times weekly ○ once a week ○ 2x/month ○ rarely ○ never ○ N/A

Comments [   ]

buy books? ○ daily ○ 2-3 times weekly ○ once a week ○ 2x/month ○ rarely ○ never ○ N/A

Comments [   ]

read stories with your child(ren)?

○ daily ○ 2-3 times weekly ○ once a week ○ 2x/month ○ rarely ○ never ○ N/A

Comments [   ]

tell stories to your child(ren)?

○ daily ○ 2-3 times weekly ○ once a week ○ 2x/month ○ rarely ○ never ○ N/A

Comments [   ]

ask about your child(ren)'s homework?

○ daily ○ 2-3 times weekly ○ once a week ○ 2x/month ○ rarely ○ never ○ N/A

Comments [   ]

help with your child(ren)'s homework?

○ daily ○ 2-3 times weekly ○ once a week ○ 2x/month ○ rarely ○ never ○ N/A

Comments [   ]

write notes/messages to your child(ren)?

○ daily ○ 2-3 times weekly ○ once a week ○ 2x/month ○ rarely ○ never ○ N/A

Comments [   ]

Approximately how many books do you have? [   ]

Approximately how many books do your children have? [   ]

Comments [   ]

In what ways do you and your family participate in your local community?

[   ]

Intergenerational Literacy Project

Learner Exit Form

Data entry date [   ]

CHILDREN'S SCHOOL PERFORMANCE

<u>Child #1</u>   Child's name [   ] ,   Grade [   ]

How would you describe your child's attitude toward school?

○ My child almost always likes to go to school.
○ My child's attitude about school changes often. Some days s/he likes it and some days s/he doesn't.
○ My child does not like school.
○ I'm not sure about my child's attitude toward school.

How does your child do in school?

○ My child always receives good grades and good reports from school.
○ My child usually receives good grades and good reports from school.
○ My child sometimes receives good grades/reports and sometimes receives poor grades/ reports from school.
○ My child usually receives poor grades and poor reports from school.
○ I am not sure how my child does in school.

How often do you communicate with your child(ren)'s teacher?

○ daily
○ once a week
○ monthly
○ a few times a year
○ never
○ (2-3 times/**week**
○ (2x/month)
○ (rarely)

In what ways do you communicate with your child's teacher?

☐ notes or letters
☐ telephone calls
☐ conferences
☐ conversations when I bring my child to or pick my child up from school

For what reasons do you contact your child's teacher?

[   ]

Comments [   ]

APPENDIX C

Writing Evaluation Rubric

Writing Evaluation Rubric

General Competence	Organization	Elaboration	Mechanics
Commendable Writer (4)	Clear development of beginning, middle, and end; logically sequenced ideas; smooth and logical transitions.	All general statements are supported by clear and specific details. All details directly support or elaborate upon general statements. Choice of words and phrases conveys rich and precise meanings.	Sentence patterns are grammatically accurate, varied, and complex; consistent use of spelling and punctuation conventions.
Adequate Writer (3)	Clear development of beginning, middle, end; logically sequenced ideas. Most transitions are logical but repetitive.	Most general statements are supported by clear and specific details. A few details are a digression from general statements. Choice of words and phrases conveys rich and precise meanings.	Sentence patterns are grammatically accurate and some are varied in complexity; consistent use of spelling and punctuation conventions.
Developing Writer (2)	Inadequate development of beginning, middle, and end; some disorganization in the sequence of ideas; few attempts to develop effective transitions.	At least one general statement is supported by clear and specific details. Several details are a digresion from general statements. Choice of vocabulary and phrases does not adequately convey precise meanings.	Sentence patterns are generally grammatically accurate but simple in structure; inconsistent use of spelling and punctuation conventions.
Beginning Writer (1)	Inadequate development of beginning, middle, end; no clear organization of ideas; no attempt to develop effective transitions.	No inclusion of specific details to support general statements. Details are unrelated to general statements. Choice of vocabulary and phrases does not adequately convey precise meanings.	Sentence patterns are often grammatically inaccurate; inconsistent use of spelling and punctuation conventions.

APPENDIX D

Teacher Seminar Readings

Teacher Seminar in Home–School Partnerships: Family Literacy Portfolio Project Readings

Ada, A. F. (1988). The Pajaro Valley experience: Working with Spanish-speaking parents to develop children's reading and writing skills in the home through use of children's literature. In T. S. Kutnabb-Kangas & J. Cummins (Eds.), *Minority education: From shame to struggle* (pp. 223–238). Philadelphia: Multilingual Matters.

Auerbach, E. R. (1989). Toward a socio-cultural approach to family literacy. *Harvard Educational Review, 59*, 165–181.

Corno, L. (1989). What it means to be literate about classrooms. In D. Bloome (Ed.), *Classrooms and literacy* (pp. 29–52). Norwood, NJ: Ablex.

Delgado-Gaitan, C. (1992). School matters in the Mexican-American home: Socializing children to education. *American Educational Research Journal, 29*, 495–513.

Delpit, L. D. (1988). The silenced dialogue: Power and pedagogy in educating other people's children. *Harvard Educational Review, 58*, 280–298.

Epstein, J. L., & Dauber, S. L. (1991). School programs and teacher practices of parent involvement in inner-city elementary and middle schools. *Elementary School Journal, 91*, 289–304.

Goldenberg, C. (1996). The education of language-minority students: Where are we, and where do we need to go? *Elementary School Journal, 96*, 353–361.

Goldenberg, C., Reese, L., & Gallimore, R. (1992). Effects of literacy materials from school on Latino children's home experience and early reading achievement. *American Journal of Education, 100*, 497–536.

Hoover-Dempsey, K. V., & Sandler, H. M. (1995). Parental involvement in children's education: Why does it make a difference? *Teacher's College Record, 97*, 310–331.

Lareau, A. (1996). Assessing parent involvement in schooling: A critical analysis. In A. Booth & F. Dunn (Eds.), *Family school links: How do they affect educational outcomes?* Mahwah, NJ: Erlbaum.

Moles, O. C. (1993). Collaboration between schools and disadvantaged parents: Obstacles and openings. In N. Chavkin (Ed.), *Families and schools in a pluralistic society* (pp. 21–52). Albany: State University of New York Press.

Moll, L. C., & Gonzalez, N. (1994). Lessons from research with language-minority children. *Journal of Reading Behavior, 26*, 439–456.

Paratore, J. R. (1994). Parents and children sharing literacy. In D. Lancy (Ed.), *Children's emergent literacy* (pp. 193–216). Westport, CT: Praeger.

Paratore, J. R. (1995). Implementing an intergenerational literacy program: Lessons learned. In L. M. Morrow (Ed.), *Family literacy: Connections in schools and communities* (pp. 37–53). Newark, DE: International Reading Association.

Paratore, J. R., Homza, A., Krol-Sinclair, B., Lewis-Barrow, T., Melzi, G., Stergis, R., & Haynes, H. (1995). Shifting boundaries in home and school responsibilities: Involving immigrant parents in the construction of literacy portfolios. *Research in the Teaching of English, 29,* 367–389.

Paratore, J. R., & Krol-Sinclair, B. (1996). A classroom storybook-reading program with immigrant parents. *School Community Journal, 6,* 39–51.

Parra, E. H., & Henderson, R. W. (1982). Mexican-American perceptions of parent and teacher roles in child development. In J. A. Fishman & G. D. Keller (Eds.), *Bilingual education for Hispanic students in the US* (pp. 289–302). New York: Teachers College Press.

Shockley, B., Michalone, B., & Allen, J. (1995). *Engaging families: Connecting home and school literacy communities.* Portsmouth, NH: Heinemann.

Taylor, D. (1993). Family literacy: Resisting the deficit hypothesis. *TESOL Quarterly, 27,* 550–553.

Valdés, G. (1996). *Con respeto: Bridging the differences between culturally diverse families and schools.* New York: Teachers College Press.

REFERENCES

Ada, A. F. (1988). The Pajaro Valley experience: Working with Spanish-speaking parents to develop children's reading and writing skills in the home through use of children's literature. In T. S. Kutnabb-Kangas & J. Cummins (Eds.), *Minority education: From shame to struggle* (pp. 223–238). Philadelphia: Multilingual Matters.

Akinnaso, F. N. (1991). Literacy and individual consciousness. In E. M. Jennings & A. C. Purves (Eds.), *Literate systems and individual lives: Perspectives on literacy and schooling* (pp. 73–94). Albany: State University of New York Press.

Allington, R. L. (1983). The reading instruction provided readers of differing abilities. *Elementary School Journal, 83,* 548–559.

Anderson, R. C., Hiebert, E. H., Scott, J., & Wilkinson, I. (1985). *Becoming a nation of readers.* Washington, DC: U.S. Department of Education, National Institute of Education.

Archbald, D. A., & Newmann, F. M. (1988). *Beyond standardized testing.* Reston, VA: National Association of School Secondary Principals.

Arnold, D. S., & Whitehurst, G. J. (1994). Accelerating language development through picture book reading: A summary of dialogic reading and its effects. In D. K. Dickinson (Ed.), *Bridges to literacy: Children, families, and schools* (pp. 103–128). Cambridge, UK: Blackwell.

Asheim, L. (1987). *The reader–viewer–listener: An essay in communication.* Washington, DC: Library of Congress.

Auerbach, E. (1997). Reading between the lines. In D. Taylor (Ed.), *Many families, many literacies* (pp. 71–81). Portsmouth, NH: Heinemann.

Auerbach, E. R. (1989). Toward a socio-cultural approach to family literacy. *Harvard Educational Review, 59,* 165–181.

Auerbach, E. R. (1992). *Making meaning, making change: Participatory curriculum development for adult ESL literacy.* Washington, DC: The Center for Applied Lingistics; McHenry, IL: Delta Systems.

Barnett, W. S. (1998). Long-term effects on cognitive development and school success. In W. S. Barnett & S. S. Boocock (Eds.), *Early care and education for children in poverty: Promise, programs, and long-term results* (pp. 11–44). Albany: State University of New York Press.

Bode, B. A. (1989). Dialogue journal writing. *Reading Teacher, 42,* 568–571.

Briggs, C., & Elkind, D. (1977). Characteristics of early readers. *Perceptual and Motor Skills, 44,* 1231–1237.

Bronfenbrenner, U. (1979). Who needs parent education? In H. J. Leichter (Ed.), *Families and communities as educators* (pp. 203–223). New York: Teachers College Press.

Brown, A. L., Armbruster, B. B., & Baker, L. (1986). The role of metacognition in reading and studying. In J. Orasanu (Ed.), *Reading comprehension: From research to practice* (pp. 49–75). Hillsdale, NJ: Erlbaum.

Bus, A. G., van Ijzendoorn, M. H. , & Pellegrini, A. D. (1995). Joint book reading makes for success in learning to read: A meta-analysis in intergenerational transmission of literacy. *Review of Educational Research, 65,* 1–21.

Chall, J. S., & Feldman, S. (1966). First-grade reading: An analysis of the interactions of professed methods, teacher implementation, and child background. *Reading Teacher, 19,* 569–575.

Chittenden, E. (1991). Authentic assessment, evaluation, and documentation of student performance. In V. Perrone (Ed.), *Expanding student assessment* (pp. 22–31). Alexandria, VA: Association for Supervision and Curriculum Development.

Clark, M. (1976). *Young fluent readers: What they can teach us.* London: Heinemann.

Clark, R. (1983). *Family life and school achievement.* Chicago: University of Chicago Press.

Clay, M. (1985). *The early detection of reading difficulties* (3rd ed.). Portsmouth, NH: Heinemann.

131

Cochran, M., & Dean, C. (1991). Home–school relations and the empowerment process. *Elementary School Journal, 91,* 261–269.

Comer, J. P. (1984). Home–school relationships as they affect the academic success of children. *Education and Urban Society, 16,* 323–337.

Comer, J. P. (1986). Parent participation in schools. *Phi Delta Kappan, 67,* 442–446.

Corno, L. (1989). What it means to be literate about classrooms. In D. Bloome (Ed.), *Classrooms and literacy* (pp. 29–52). Norwood, NJ: Ablex.

Cuckle, P. (1996). Children learning to read—exploring home and school relationships. *British Educational Research Journal, 22,* 17–32.

Darling, S. (1997). *Opening session speech.* Paper presented at the sixth annual Conference on Family Literacy, Louisville, KY.

Darling, S., & Hayes, A. (1988–89). *Family literacy project final project report.* Louisville, KY: National Center for Family Literacy.

Davies, D. (1996). *Partnerships for student success.* Baltimore, MD.: Johns Hopkins University Center on Families, Communities, Schools, and Children's Learning.

Degener, S. C. (1998). *Critical literacy theory in family literacy: What difference does it make?* Unpublished manuscript, Harvard Graduate School of Education.

Delgado-Gaitan, C. (1990). *Literacy for empowerment: The role of parents in children's education.* New York: Falmer Press.

Delgado-Gaitan, C. (1992). School matters in the Mexican-American home: Socializing children to education. *American Educational Research Journal, 29,* 495–513.

Delgado-Gaitan, C. (1993). Research and policy in reconceptualizing family–school relationships. In P. Phelan & A. Locke-Davidson (Eds.), *Renegotiating cultural diversity in American schools* (pp. 139–158). New York: Teachers College Press.

Delgado-Gaitan, C. (1994). Spanish speaking families' involvement in schools. In C. L. Fagnano & B. Z. Werber (Eds.), *School, family and community interaction: A view from the firing lines* (pp. 85–98). Boulder, CO: Westview.

Delgado-Gaitan, C. (1996). *Protean literacy: Extending the discourse on empowerment.* New York: Falmer Press.

Delpit, L. (1995). *Other people's children: Cultural conflict in the classroom.* New York: New Press.

Diaz, R. (1983). Thought and two languages: The impact of bilingualism on cognitive development. In E. W. Gordon (Ed.), *Review of research in education* (Vol. 10, pp. 23–54). Washington, DC: American Educational Research Association.

Diaz, S., Moll, L. C., & Mehan, H. (1986). Sociocultural resources in instruction: A context-specific approach. In *Beyond language: Social and cultural factors in schooling language minority students* (pp. 187–230). Los Angeles: California State University, Evaluation, Dissemination, and Assessment Center.

Donahue, P. L., Voelkl, K. E., Campbell, J. R., & Mazzeo, J. (1999). *NAEP 1998: Reading report card for the nation.* Washington, DC: U.S. Department of Education, Office of Educational Research and Improvement, National Center for Education Statistics.

Dunn, N. E. (1981). Children's achievement at school-entry age as a function of mothers' and fathers' teaching sets. *Elementary School Journal, 81,* 245–253.

Duran, R. A. (1996). English immigrant language learners: Cultural accommodation and family literacy. In L. A. Benjamin & J. Lord (Eds.), *Family literacy: Directions in research and implications for practice* (pp. 25–30). Washington, DC: U.S. Department of Education, Office of Educational Research and Improvement.

Durkin, D. (1966). *Children who read early.* New York: Teachers College Press.

Dweck, C. S. (1986). Motivational processes affecting learning. *American Psychologist, 41,* 1040–1048.

Eder, D. (1983). Ability grouping and students' academic self-concepts: A case study. *Elementary School Journal, 84,* 149–161.

Edmondson, J., & Shannon, P. (1998). Reading education and poverty: Questioning the reading success equation. *Peabody Journal of Education, 73,* 104–126.

Edwards, P. A. (1991). Fostering early literacy through parent coaching. In E. Hiebert (Ed.), *Literacy for a diverse society* (pp. 199–213). New York: Teachers College Press.

Epstein, J. (1986). Parents' reactions to teacher practices of parent involvement. *Elementary School Journal, 86,* 277–294.

Epstein, J. (1994). Theory to practice: School and family relationships lead to school improvement and student success. In C. L. Fagnano & B. Z. Werber (Eds.), *School, family, and community interaction* (pp. 39–54). Boulder, CO: Westview.

Epstein, J. L., & Dauber, S. L. (1991). School programs and teacher practices of parent involvement in inner-city elementary and middle schools. *Elementary School Journal, 91,* 289–304.

Farkas, S., Johnson, J., Duffett, A., Aulicino, C., & McHugh, J. (1999). *Playing their parts: Parents and teachers talk about parental involvement in public schools.* New York: Public Agenda.

Ferdman, B. (1990). Literacy and cultural identity. *Harvard Educational Review, 60,* 181–204.

Fisher, C. W., Filby, N. N., Marliave, R., Cahen, L. S., Dishaw, M. M., Moore, J. E., & Berliner, D. C. (1978). *Teaching behaviors, academic learning time, and student achievement: Final report of phase III-B, beginning teacher evaluation study.* San Francisco: Far West Educational Laboratory for Educational Research and Development.

Flavell, J. H. (1979). Metacognition and cognitive monitorings: A new area of cognitive–developmental inquiry. *American Psychologist, 334,* 906–911.

Flavell, J. H., & Wellman, H. M. (1977). Metamemory. In J. R. V. Kail & J. W. Hagen (Eds.), *Perspectives on the development of memory and cognition* (pp. 3–33). Hillsdale, NJ: Erlbaum.

Florio-Ruane, S. (1987). Sociolinguistics for educational researchers. *American Educational Research Journal, 24,* 185–197.

Foster, M. (1993). Educating for competence in community and culture. *Urban Education, 27,* 370–394.

Freire, P. (1970). *Pedagogy of the oppressed.* New York: Continuum.

Gadsden, V. (1994). *Understanding family literacy: Conceptual issues facing the field.* Philadelphia: University of Pennsylvania National Center for Adult Literacy.

Galindo, R., & Escamilla, E. (1995). A biographical perspective on Chicano educational success. *Urban Review, 27,* 1–29.

Garcia, E. E. (1988). Attributes of effective schools for language minority students. *Education and Urban Society, 20,* 387–398.

Gaudet, R. D. (2000). *Effective school districts in Massachusetts: A study of student performance on the 1999 MCAS Assessments.* Amherst: University of Massachusetts, Donahue Institute.

Gee, J. P. (1989). What is literacy? *Journal of Education, 171,* 18–25.

Gee, J. P. (1999). Critical issues: Reading and the new literacy studies: Reframing the National Academy of Sciences report on reading. *Journal of Literacy Research, 31,* 355–374.

Getzels, J. W. (1974). Socialization and education: A note on discontinuities. *Teachers College Record, 76,* 218–225.

Goldenberg, C. (1987). Low income Hispanic parents' contributions to their first-grade children's word-recognition skills. *Anthropology and Education Quarterly, 18,* 149–179.

Goldenberg, C. (1992–93). Instructional conversations: Promoting comprehension through discussion. *Reading Teacher, 46,* 316–326.

Goldenberg, C. (1996). The education of language-minority students: Where are we, and where do we need to go? *Elementary School Journal, 96,* 353–361.

Gonzalez, N., Moll, L. C., Tenery, M. F., Rivera, A., Rendon, P., Gonzales, R., & Amanti, C. (1995). Funds of knowledge for teaching in Latino households. *Urban Education, 29,* 443–470.

Good, T. L., & Marshall, S. (1984). Do students learn more in heterogeneous or homogeneous groups? In P. L. Peterson, L. C. Wilkinson, & M. Hallinan (Eds.), *The social context of instruction: Group organization and group processes* (pp. 15–38). New York: Academic Press.

Greenes, C. E. (1994). The Boston University/Chelsea public schools partnership: The history: 1986–1994. *Journal of Education, 176,* 9–20.

Gundlach, R. (1992). What it means to be literate. In R. Beach, J. L. Green, M. L. Kamil, & T. Shanahan (Eds.), *Multidisciplinary perspectives on literacy research* (pp. 365–372). Urbana, IL: National Conference on Research in English and National Council of Teachers of English.

Hakuta, K. (1986). *Mirror of language.* New York: Basic Books.

Harris, T. L., & Hodges, R. E. (1995). *The literacy dictionary.* Newark, DE: International Reading Association.

Harry, B. (1992). *Cultural diversity, families, and the special education system.* New York: Teachers College Press.

Heath, S. B. (1983). *Ways with words.* Cambridge: Cambridge University Press.

Henderson, A. T., & Berla, N. (Eds.). (1994). *A new generation of evidence: The family is critical to student achievement.* Washington, DC: Center for Law and Education.

Hendrix, S. (1999). Family literacy education—Panacea or false promise? *Journal of Adolescent & Adult Literacy, 43,* 338–357.

Hiebert, E. H. (1983). An examination of ability grouping for reading instruction. *Reading Research Quarterly, 18,* 231–255.

Hoover-Dempsey, K. V., & Sandler, H. M. (1997). Why do parents become involved in their children's education? *Review of Educational Research, 67,* 3–42.

Huey, E. B. (1908). *The psychology and pedagogy of reading.* Cambridge, MA: MIT Press.

Intergenerational Literacy Project. (1994). *Stories we share.* Boston: Boston University/Chelsea Public Schools Intergenerational Literacy Project.

Intergenerational Literacy Project. (1995). *Sharing our stories.* Boston: Boston University/Chelsea Public Schools Intergenerational Literacy Project.

Intergenerational Literacy Project. (1996). *Sharing our stories.* Boston: Boston University/Chelsea Public Schools Intergenerational Literacy Project.

Intergenerational Literacy Project. (1998). *Our lives, our dreams.* Boston: Boston University/Chelsea Public Schools Intergenerational Literacy Project.

Intergenerational Literacy Project. (1999). *Life and learning.* Boston: Boston University/Chelsea Public Schools Intergenerational Literacy Project.

International Reading Association. (1999). High stakes assessments in reading: A position statement of the International Reading Association. *Reading Teacher, 53,* 257–264.

Jiménez, R., & Gersten, R. (1999). Lessons and dilemmas derived from the literacy instruction of two Latina/o teachers. *American Educational Research Journal, 36,* 265–302.

Johnson, D. W., Maruyama, G., Johnson, R., & Nelson, D. (1981). Effects of cooperative, competitive, and individualistic goal structures: A meta-analysis. *Psychological Bulletin, 89,* 47–62.

Johnston, P. (1997). Standardized tests in family literacy programs. In D. Taylor (Ed.), *Many families, many literacies* (pp. 142–148). Portsmouth, NH: Heinemann.

Johnston, P., & Allington, R. (1991). Remediation. In R. Barr, M. L. Kamil, P. G. Mosenthal, & P. D. Pearson (Eds.), *Handbook of reading research* (Vol. 2, pp. 984–1012). New York: Longman.

Kreeft-Peyton, J. (1986). Literacy through written interaction. *Passages, 2,* 24–29.

Krol-Sinclair, B. (1996). Connecting home and school literacies: Immigrant parents with limited formal education as classroom storybook readers. In D. J. Leu, C. K. Kinzer, & K. A. Hinchman (Eds.), *Literacies for the 21st Century: Research and practice* (pp. 270–283). Chicago: National Reading Conference.

Lankshear, C., & O'Connor, P. (1999). Response to adult literacy: The next generation. *Educational Researcher, 28,* 30–36.

Lareau, A. (1987). Social class differences in family–school relationships: The importance of cultural capital. *Sociology of Education, 60,* 73–85.

Lareau, A. (1989). *Home advantage: Social class and parental intervention.* New York: Falmer Press.

Lareau, A. (1994). Parent involvement in schooling: A dissenting view. In C. L. Fagnano & B. Z. Werber (Eds.), *School, family, in community interaction: A view from the firing lines* (pp. 61–73). Boulder, CO: Westview.

Logan, B. (1999). Parent and child together (PACT) time in elementary schools. In *Momentum: National Center for Family Literacy.* Louisville, KY: National Center for Family Literacy.

Lynch, E. W., & Stein, R. C. (1987). Parent participation by ethnicity. *Exceptional Children, 54,* 105–111.

Mason, J. M. (1980). When do children begin to read: An exploration of four year old children's letter and word reading competencies. *Reading Research Quarterly, 15,* 203–227.

McCarthey, S. J. (1997). Connecting home and school literacy practices in classrooms with diverse populations. *Journal of Literacy Research, 29,* 145–182.

McMahon, S. I., Raphael, T. E., Goatley, V., & Pardo, L. (1997). *The book club connection: Literacy learning and classroom talk.* Newark, DE: International Reading Association.

Mehan, H., Villanueva, I., Hubbard, L., & Lintz, A. (1996). *Constructing school success: The consequences of untracking low-achieving students.* New York: Cambridge University Press.

Moll, L. C. (1992). Literacy research in community and classrooms: A sociocultural approach. In R. Beach, J. L. Green, M. L. Kamil, & T. Shanahan (Eds.), *Multidisciplinary perspectives in literacy research* (pp. 211–244). Urbana, IL: National Council of Teachers of English.

Moll, L. C. (1998). Turning to the world: Bilingual schooling, literacy, and the cultural mediation of thinking. *National Reading Conference Yearbook, 47,* 59–75.

Moll, L. C., & Greenberg, J. B. (1992). Creating zones of possibilities: Combining social contexts for instruction. In L. C. Moll (Ed.), *Vygotsky in Education* (pp. 319–348). New York: Cambridge University Press.

Moll, L. C., Amanti, C., Neff, D., & Gonzalez, N. (1992). Funds of knowledge for teaching: Using a qualitative approach to connect homes and classrooms. *Theory into Practice, 31,* 132–141.

Moran, C. E., & Hakuta, K. (1995). Bilingual education: Broadening research perspectives. In J. A. Banks & C. A. M. Banks (Eds.), *Handbook of research on multicultural education* (pp. 445–464). New York: Macmillan.

Morrow, L. M. (1983). Home and school correlates of early interest in literature. *Journal of Educational Research, 76,* 221–230.

Morrow, L. M., Paratore, J. R., Gaber, D., Harrison, D., & Tracey, D. (1993). Family literacy perspective and practices. *Reading Teacher, 47,* 194–200.

Murphy, S. (1997). Who's reading whose reading? The National Center for Family Literacy evaluation process. In D. Taylor (Ed.), *Many families, many literacies* (pp. 149–151). Portsmouth, NH: Heinemann.

National Center for Children in Poverty. (1999). High school diploma, working parents, little protection against young child poverty. *News and Issues,* p. 3.

National Center for Education Statistics (1998). *Parent involvement in children's education: Efforts by public elementary schools* (NCES 98–032). Washington, DC: National Center for Education Statistics, U.S. Department of Education.

National Center for Education Statistics (1999a). *The condition of education.* Washington, DC: National Center for Education Statistics, U.S. Department of Education.

National Center for Education Statistics. (1999b). *Education statistics quarterly,* (vol. 1). Washington, DC: National Center for Education Statistics, U.S. Department of Education.

National Center for Family Literacy. (nd). *The power of family literacy.* Louisville, KY: Author.

The New London Group. (1996). A pedagogy of multiliteracies: Designing social futures. *Harvard Educational Review, 66,* 60–92.

Oakes, J. (1985). *Keeping track: How schools structure inequality.* New Haven: Yale University Press.

Office of Governmental and Interagency Affairs. (1996). Secretary Riley defines education challenges, urges Americans to come together. *Community Update, 33,* 1, 6.

Orfield, G., & Yun, J. T. (1999). *Resegregation in American schools* (<http://www.law.harvard.edu/groups/civilrights/publications/resegregation99.html>). Cambridge, MA: The Civil Rights Project, Harvard University.

Palmer, D. J., & Goetz, E. T. (1988). Studier's beliefs about self and strategies. In C. E. Weinstein, E. T. Goetz, & P. A. Alexander (Eds.), *Learning and study strategies: Issues in assessment, instruction, and evaluation* (pp. 41–61). New York: Academic Press.

Paratore, J. R. (1991). *Flexible grouping: Why and how?* Needham, MA: Silver Burdett Ginn.

Paratore, J. R. (1993). Influence of an intergenerational approach to literacy on the practice of literacy of parents and their children. In C. Kinzer & D. Leu (Eds.), *Examining central issues in literacy, research, theory, and practice* (pp. 83–91). Chicago: National Reading Conference.

Paratore, J. R. (1994). Parents and children sharing literacy. In D. Lancy (Ed.), *Children's emergent literacy* (pp. 193–216). Westport, CT: Praeger.

Paratore, J. R., Hindin, A., Krol-Sinclair, B., & Durán, P. (1999). Discourse between teachers and Latino parents during conferences based on home literacy portfolios. *Education and Urban Society, 32,* 58–82.

Paratore, J. R., Hindin, A., Krol-Sinclair, B., Durán, P., & Emig, J. (1999). *Deepening the conversation: Using family literacy portfolios as a context for parent–teacher conferences.* Paper presented at the National Reading Conference, Orlando, FL.

Paratore, J. R., Homza, A., Krol-Sinclair, B., Lewis-Barrow, T., Melzi, G., Stergis, R., & Haynes, H. (1995). Shifting boundaries in home and school responsibilities: Involving immigrant parents in the construction of literacy portfolios. *Research in the Teaching of English, 29*, 367–389.

Paratore, J. R., & Krol-Sinclair, B. (1996). A classroom storybook-reading program with immigrant parents. *School Community Journal, 6*, 39–51.

Paratore, J. R., Melzi, G., & Krol-Sinclair, B. (1999). *What should we expect of family literacy? Experiences of Latino children whose parents participate in an intergenerational literacy program.* Newark, DE: International Reading Association.

Paris, S. G., Lipson, M. Y., & Wixson, K. K. (1983). Becoming a strategic reader. *Contemporary Educational Psychology, 8*, 293–316.

Paris, S. G., Wasik, B. A., & Turner, J. C. (1991). The development of strategic readers. In R. Barr, M. L. Kamiil, P. B. Mosenthal, & P. D. Pearson (Eds.), *Handbook of reading research* (Vol. 2, pp. 609–640). New York: Longman.

Parra, E. & Henderson, R. W. (1982). *Mexican-American perceptions of parent and teacher roles in child development.* In J. A. Fishman & G. D. Keller (Eds.), *Bilingual education for Hispanic students in the US* (pp. 289–302). New York: Teachers College Press.

Pearson, P. D., & Gallagher, M. C. (1983). The instruction of reading comprehension. *Contemporary Educational Psychology, 8*, 317–344.

Pressley, M. (1998). Comprehension strategies instruction. In J. Osborn & F. Lehr (Eds.), *Literacy for all* (pp. 113–133). New York: Guilford Press.

Purcell-Gates, V. (1993). Issues for family literacy research: Voices from the teachers. *Language Arts, 70*, 670–677.

Purcell-Gates, V. (1995). *Other people's words: The cycle of illiteracy.* Cambridge: Harvard University Press.

Purcell-Gates, V. (1996). Stories, coupons, and the TV Guide: Relationships between home literacy experiences and emergent literacy knowledge. *Reading Research Quarterly, 31*, 406–428.

Purves, A. C. (1991). The textual contract: Literacy as common knowledge and conventional wisdom. In E. M. Jennings & A. C. Purves (Eds.), *Literate systems and individual lives* (pp. 51–72). Albany: State University of New York Press.

Quintero, E., & Huerto-Macías, A. (1990). All in the family: Bilingualism and biliteracy. *Reading Teacher, 44*, 306–312.

Quintero, E., & Velarde, M. C. (1990). Intergenerational literacy: A developmental bilingual approach. *Young Children, 45*, 10–15.

Radencich, M. C., & McKay, L. J. (1995). *Flexible grouping for literacy in the elementary school.* Boston: Allyn and Bacon.

Radencich, M. C., McKay, L. J., Paratore, J. R., Plaza, G. L., Lustgarten, K. E., Nelms, O., & Moore, P. T. (1995). Implementing flexible grouping with a common reading selection. In M. C. Radencich & L. J. McKay (Eds.), *Flexible grouping for literacy in the elementary grades* (pp. 25–41). Boston: Allyn and Bacon.

Rodgríuez-Brown, F. V., Li, R. F., & Albom, J. A. (1999). Hispanic parents' awareness and use of literacy-rich environments at home and in the community. *Education and Urban Society, 32*, 41–57.

Sable, J., & Stennett, J. (1998). *The educational progress of Hispanic students.* Washington, DC: National Center for Education Statistics, U.S. Department of Education.

Scarborough, H. S., & Dobrich, W. (1994). On the efficacy of reading to preschoolers. *Developmental Review, 14*, 245–302.

Schieffelin, B., & Cochran-Smith, M. (1984). Learning to read culturally: Literacy before schooling. In H. Goelman, A. Oberg, & F. Smith (Eds.), *Awakening to literacy* (pp. 3–23). Exeter, NH: Heinemann.

Scribner, S. (1986). Literacy in three metaphors. In N. L. Stein (Ed.), *Literacy in American schools* (pp. 7–22). Chicago: University of Chicago Press.

Sears, D. (1994). The Boston University/Chelsea public schools partnership: The Present. *Journal of Education, 176*, 21–28.

Secada, W. G., Chavez-Chavez, R., Garcia, E., Muñoz, C., Oakes, J., Santiago-Santiago, I., & Slavin, R. (1998). *No more excuses: The final report of the Hispanic dropout project.* University of Wisconsin–Madison Hispanic Dropout Project.

Segal, M. (1985). A study of maternal beliefs and values within the context of an intervention program. In I. E. Sigel (Ed.), *Parental belief systems: The psychological consequences for children* (pp. 271–286). Hillsdale, NJ: Erlbaum.

Serpell, R. (1997). Critical issues: Literacy connections between school and home: How should we evaluate them? *Journal of Literacy Research, 29,* 587–616.

Shanahan, T., Mulhern, M., & Rodriguez-Brown, F. (1995). Project FLAME: Lessons learned from a family literacy program for minority families. *Reading Teacher, 48,* 40–47.

Sharan, S. (1980). Cooperative learning in small groups: Recent methods and effects on achievement, attitudes, and ethnic relations. *Review of Educational Research, 50,* 241–271.

Shockley, B., Michalove, B., & Allen, J. (1995). *Engaging families: Connecting home and school literacy communities.* Portsmouth, NH: Heinemann.

Silber, J. (1994). The Boston University/Chelsea public schools partnership: The vision. *Journal of Education, 176,* 3–8.

Slavin, R. E. (1980). Cooperative learning. *Review of Educational Research, 50,* 315–342.

Slavin, R. E. (1987). *Ability grouping and student achievement in elementary school: A best evidence synthesis.* Baltimore: Center for Research on Elementary and Secondary Schools, Johns Hopkins University.

St. Pierre, R. G., Layzer, J. I., & Barnes, H. V. (1998). Regenerating two-generation programs. In W. S. Barnett & S. S. Boocock (Eds.), *Early care and education for children in poverty: Promises, programs, and long-term results* (pp. 99–122). Albany: State University of New York Press.

Sticht, T. G. (1988/89). Adult literacy education. *Review of Research in Education, 15,* 59–96.

Sticht, T. G., & McDonald, B. (1989). *Making the nation smarter: The intergenerational transfer of literacy.* San Diego, CA: Institute for Adult Literacy.

Sticht, T. G., Beeler, M. J., & McDonald, B. A. (Eds.). (1992). *The intergenerational transfer of cognitive skills: Vol. 2. Theory and research in cognitive science.* Norwood, NJ: Ablex.

Sticht, T. G., & McDonald, B. A. (1992). The intergenerational transfer of cognitive skills. In T. G. Sticht, M. J. Beeler, & B. A. McDonald (Eds.), *The intergenerational transfer of cognitive skills, Vol. 2, Theory and research in cognitive science* (pp. 1–13). Norwood, NJ: Ablex.

Street, B. (1995). *Social literacies: Critical approaches to literacy in development, ethnography, and education.* New York: Longman.

Suro, R. (1990, April 11). Cavazos criticizes Hispanic parents on schooling. *The New York Times,* B8.

Swadener, B. B., & Lubeck, S. (Eds.). (1995). *Children and families "at promise."* Albany: State University of New York Press.

Swanson, B. B. (1985). Listening to students about reading. *Reading Horizons, 25,* 123–128.

Swap, S. M. (1993). *Developing home-school partnerships: From concepts to practice.* New York: Teachers College Press.

Tao, F., Swartz, J., St. Pierre, R., & Tarr, H. (1997). National Evaluation of the Even Start family literacy program. Washington, DC: U.S. Department of Education Planning and Evaluation Service.

Taylor, D. (1983). *Family literacy: Young children learning to read and write.* Exeter, NH: Heinemann.

Taylor, D. (1993). Family literacy: Resisting the deficit hypothesis. *TESOL Quarterly, 27,* 550–553.

Taylor, D. (1997). *Many families, many literacies.* Portsmouth, NH: Heinemann.

Taylor, D., & Dorsey-Gaines, C. (1988). *Growing up literate: Learning from inner-city families.* Portsmouth, NH: Heinemann.

Taylor, D., & Strickland, D. (1989). Learning from families: Implications for educators and policy. In J. B. Allen & J. M. Mason (Eds.), *Risk makers, risk takers, risk breakers: Reducing the risks for young literacy learners* (pp. 251–280). Portsmouth, NH: Heinemann.

Tharp, R. G., & Gallimore, R. (1988). *Rousing minds to life.* New York: Cambridge University Press.

Thornburg, D. G. (1993). Intergenerational literacy learning with bilingual families: A contact for the analysis of social mediation of thought. *Journal of Reading Behavior, 25,* 323–352.

Tierney, R. J., Carter, M. A., & Desai, L. E. (1991). *Portfolio assessment in the reading-writing classroom.* Norwood, MA: Christopher-Gordon.

Valdés, G. (1996). *Con respeto: Bridging the differences between culturally diverse families and schools.* New York: Teachers College Press.

Vasquez, O., Pease-Alvarez, L., & Shannon, S. M. (1994). *Pushing boundaries: Language and culture in a Mexicano community.* New York: Cambridge University Press.

Vélez-Ibánez, C. G., & Greenberg, J. B. (1992). Formation and transformation of funds of knowledge among U.S.–Mexican households. *Anthropology and Education Quarterly, 23,* 313–335.

Venezky, R. L., & Winfield, L. (1979). *Schools that succeed beyond expectations in teaching reading* (Tech. Rep. No. 1). Newark, DE: University of Delaware Studies on Education.

Vygotsky, L. S. (1978). *Mind in society.* Cambridge: Harvard University Press.

Wagner, D. (1991). Literacy as culture: Emic and etic perspectives. In E. M. Jennings & A. C. Purves (Eds.), *Literate systems and individual lives: Perspectives on literacy and schooling* (pp. 11–22). Albany: State University of New York Press.

Weber, R. M. (1991). Linguistic diversity and reading in American society. In R. Barr, M. K. Kamil, P. B. Mosenthal, & P. D. Pearson (Eds.), *Handbook of reading research* (Vol. 2, pp. 97–119). New York: Longman.

Wolf, D. P. (1989). Portfolio assessment: Sampling student work. *Educational Leadership, 46*(7): 35–39.

Workforce Investment Act of 1998, Pub. L. No. 105–220, S 203, 112 Stat. 1061 (1998).

INDEX

A

Achievement
  factors in success in early
    reading, 46
  parents' report of children's
    school, 67
  rates of poor/minority
    children, 2
  reasons for higher, 2
  reasons for low, 1–2, 12
  teachers' reports of children's,
    66
Ada, A. F., 18
Adult Education and Family
  Literacy Act, 101
Adult learners, 25, 33
Adult literacy
  learning about, 100–103
  support of, 35, 38, 44–51
Akinnaso, F. N., 5
Albom, J. A., 18
Allen, J., 88, 112
Allington, R., 10, 108
Amanti, C., 14, 29, 87, 103
Amplifying function of biliterate-
  bicultural approach, 25
Anderson, R. C., 28, 46
Approaches to instruction,
  107
Archbald, D. A., 30, 55
Armbruster, B. B., 27
Arnold D. S., 29
Asheim, L., 5
Assessment
  definitions, 30, 56
  of ILP effectiveness, 52
  ILP's stance toward, 55–56
  ongoing, 34
  purpose of, 23
Assessment design, 55
Assessment measures used in ILP,
  54–56, 58–59, 81

Attendance rates, 56, 62
Audiotapes of parent-child read-
  alouds, 91
Auerbach, E., 4, 18, 23, 24,
  104–105
Aulicino, C., 83
Authentic assessment, 30

B

Baker, L., 27
Barnes, H. V., 1
Beeler, M. J., 2
Berla, N., 83
Berliner, D. C., 33
Biculturalism, 14, 22, 107
Bilingualism, 14, 107
Biliteracy, 14, 22, 107
Bode, B. A., 44
Boston University Chelsea School
  Partnership, 21–30, 31. *See
  also* Intergenerational Literacy
  Project (ILP)
Boston University study of ILP,
  19–20
Boundaries between school/ parent
  roles, 12
Brennan, J., 19
Briggs, C., 28
Bronfenbrenner, U., 6–7
Brown, A. L., 27
Bus, A. G., 28, 46

C

Cahen, L. S., 33
Campbell, J. R., 1
Carter, M. A., 30
Case studies. *See also* Research
  studies
  Hung Mei, 70–76
  Maritza, 67–70
  results of, 58–59
  Roadville/Trackton, 11

  Silvia, 76–80
  summary of, 80–81
Cavazos, L., 110
Cazden, C., 5
Centers, ILP organization by, 49
Chall, J. S., 33
Change, causes of, 105
Characteristics
  family and school, 59
  of home-school partnerships,
    88
  rationale for ILP's, 107–108
Chavez-Chavez, R., 1
Chelsea, City of, overview of,
  20–21. *See also* Intergenerational Literacy Project
  (ILP)
Chelsea School Committee, 19
Children. *See also* Research studies
  achievement rates of
    poor/minority, 2
  acknowledgment by teachers of
    literacies of, 29
  changes in literacy of, 64–67
  development of literacy of, 51
  early versus nonearly readers, 28
  interaction of in Mexican
    American families, 11–12
  language learning experiences of,
    15
  National Center for Children in
    Poverty, 2
  predictive value of factors for
    success, 111
  role of parents in learning,
    109
  role of parents in reading,
    27–28
  schoolage, who attend ILP,
    50–51
  and school literacy, learning
    about, 108–109

Children (*continued*)
  sources of school difficulties, 46
  support of learning through ILP, 48–49
Chittendon, E., 30
Clark, M., 28, 46, 85
Classroom, social issues in the, 105
Classroom literacy, 33, 92
Clay, M., 56
Cochran, M., 86, 87
Cochran-Smith, M., 24
Cognitively-oriented instruction, 27, 34
Collaboration, growth of, 112
Comer, J. P., 84, 86–87
Commission on Reading, 28
Commonalities of ILP participants, 81
Community profile of ILP participants, 19–21
Community relationships, developing, 31–32
Comprehension, methods for improving, 27
Conditional knowledge, 39
Congruence, lack of between family use of literacy and school assessment of, 54
Con Respeto (Valdés), 95
Conversation. *See* Instructional conversation
Cooperative grouping, 25–26
Corno, L., 33, 92
Countries of origin of ILP participants, 60–61
Cuckle, P., 85
Curriculum materials, 24, 35
Curriculums, ILP's, 106

D
Daily activities, 24, 35
Darling, S., 2, 16, 100
Data sources for ILP outcomes studies, 61
Dauber, S. L., 84
Davies, D., 87
Dean, C., 86, 87
Definitions
  assessment, 30, 56
  family literacy, 3
  Latino households, 14
  literacy, 4–7, 101, 103

literate persons, 101–102
multiliteracies, 5
parent involvement, 84
reading strategies, 26
Degener, S. C., 106
Delgado-Gaitan, C., 9–10, 10–11, 15, 17, 29, 54–55, 85, 110
Delpit, L., 18
Demographics of City of Chelsea, 20–21
Desai, L. E., 30
Development of children's literacy, 51
Development of community relations, 31–32
Dialogue journal responses, example, 74
Diaz, R., 18, 24
Differently literate, 15, 103
Discontinuity perspective, 14
Dishaw, M. M., 33
Dobrich, W., 28
Donahue, P. L., 1
Dorsey-Gaines, C., 9, 15, 29, 110
Duffet, A., 83
Dunn, N. E., 28
Durán, P., 95
Duran, R. A., 22, 23
Durkin, D., 28, 46
Dweck, C. S., 25

E
Early intervention programs, effects of, 15–16
Eder, D., 25
Edmondson, J., 100, 104
Educational principles of ILP, 21–30, 34
Edwards, P. A., 85
Elkind, D., 28
Emig, J., 95
Epstein, J., 84, 85, 86, 111
Escamilla, E., 85
Ethnographies, 7, 14. *See also* Case studies; Research studies
Evaluation program, ILP's, 53–54
Even Start program, 107
Examples
  dialogue journal responses, 74
  journal entries, 41, 73
  learner exit interview, 121–125
  learner intake interview, 114–119

literacy logs, 36–37, 79
writing evaluation rubric, 128
Exit interviews, 30, 56, 109, 121–125

F
Families
  countries of origin of ILP, 60–61
  of different cultures/languages, commonalities between, 13
  recruiting for Intergenerational Literacy Project (ILP), 32
  served by ILP, 57–58
Family activities suggestions, 50
Family-based intervention programs, effects of, 54–55
Family intervention programs, 13
Family literacy
  attempts to quiet the noise about, 100
  definition, 3
  divide in the field of, 16
  learning about, 100–103
  obstacles to investigators of, 54
  supporting, 35
Family literacy portfolio, 93
Family literacy practices, 63, 64
Family literacy programs
  characteristics of participants, 103
  disagreements in, 16–17
  evidence of legitimacy of, 17–18
  key assumptions of, 18
  learning about, 104–108
  reciprocity in, 2
Farkas, S., 83
Feldman, S., 33
Ferdman, B., 5
Filby, N. N., 33
Fisher, C. W., 33
Flavell, J. H., 27
Flexible grouping model, 38
Florio-Ruane, S., 46
Formal strategies, 102–103
Foster, M., 103
Freire, P., 104–105
Funding sources for ILP, 52n1
Funds of knowledge, 14

G
Gaber, D., 100
Gadsden, V., 1, 16–17

Galindo, R., 85
Gallagher, M. C., 39
Gallimore, R., 26, 39, 107
Garcia, E. E., 1, 24, 25
Gaudet, R. D., 21
Gee, J. P., 5, 6, 16, 24
Gersten, R., 26, 27
Getzels, J. W., 87
Goals
  disagreements about, 100
  of ILP, 19, 35
  model goals of National Center
    for Family Literacy, 16
  questions raised for family
    literacy intervention, 109
Goatley, V., 51
Goetz, E. T., 27
Goldenberg, C., 24, 26, 39, 85, 107
Gonzales, R., 14, 18
Gonzalez, N., 29, 87, 103
Good, T. L., 25
Greenburg, J. B., 18, 87
Greenes, C. E., 20
Grouping practices in literacy
    learning
  cooperative, 25–26
  flexible grouping model, 26, 38
  grouping students by reading
    proficiency, 25–26
  heterogeneous, 25–26
  heterogeneous instructional
    groups, 22
  homogeneous grouping, 107
  minority group socialization
    practices, 13
Groups, forming multilingual/
    multicultural, 107
Group socialization practices, 13
Guiding educational principles of
    ILP, 21–30, 34
Gundlach, R., 103

H
Hakuta, K., 24
Harris, T. L., 30
Harrison, D., 100
Harry, B., 15
Hayes, A., 16, 100
Heath, S. B., 8, 15, 110
Henderson, A. T., 83, 85
Hendrix, S., 2
Heterogeneous classes, 34, 107

Hiebert, E. H., 10, 25, 28, 46
Hindin, A., 95
Hispanic parents, 110
Hodges, R. E., 30
Home-Rule Bill (Massachusetts),
  19–20
Home-school communication,
  10–11
Home-School Literacy Portfolio
  Project, 92–98
Home-school partnerships
  Home-School Literacy Portfolio
    Project, 92–98
  initiatives, 88
  learning about, 109–111
  Parents as Classroom Storybook
    Readers Project, 89–92
Home-School Portfolio Project,
  110
Homework, role of in home
  literacy, 10
Homogeneous grouping, 107
Hoover-Dempsey, K. V., 84
Household networks, 14–15
Hubbard, L., 15
Huerto-Macías, A., 18
Huey, E. B., 27–28
Hung Mei (case study), 70–76

I
Informal strategies, 102–103
Instruction
  building upon biliterate-
    bicultural backgrounds, 34
  cognitively oriented, 22
  explicit, 39
Instructional conversation, 26,
  39–40
Instructional cycles of ILP, 34
Instructional groups, heterogeneous, 22
Intake interviews, 30, 56, 114–119
Intergenerational Literacy Project
  (ILP)
  about the community, 19–21
  assessment design, 55
  cited works/studies, 40, 43, 46,
    50, 101, 102, 104
  daily activities, 35
  development of community
    relations, 31–32
  family activities suggestions, 50

flexible grouping and
  instructional framework for
  reading lessons, 38
funding sources, 52n1
goals of, 19
guiding educational principles
  of, 21–30, 34
instructional cycles, 34
journal entry example, 41
monitoring learning, 51–52
origins of, 18
printed label for child's school
  record, 51
purpose of, 88–89
reading lessons, 35, 38–39
recruiting families, 32
securing a site for, 32–33
self-monitoring, 44–51
summary of findings, 81–82
writing lessons, 41–44
International Reading Association,
  56

J
Jiménez, R., 26, 27
Johnson, D. W., 25, 83
Johnston, P., 100, 108
Journal entries, 40, 41, 73

K
Keats, E. J., 49
Knowledge, 14, 39
Kreeft-Peyton, J., 44
Krol-Sinclair, B., 59, 89, 91, 95,
  108

L
Language
  development/use, 49–50
  first, spoken by ILP families,
    61
  learning experiences of children,
    15
Lankshear, C., 5
Lareau, A., 15, 84–85, 112
Latino households, definition, 14
Layzer, J. I., 1
Learner exit interview (sample),
  121–125
Learner intake interview (sample),
  114–119
Learners, adult, 25

Learners, characteristics of successful versus moderate, 59–60

Learning, monitoring, 51–52

Learning outcomes, 58–67

Lessons learned, 111–112

Li, R. F., 18

Lintz, A., 15

Lipson, M. Y., 39

Literacy. *See also* Differently literate
changes in parents'/children's, 63–67
definitions, 4–7, 101, 103
as sociocultural process, 34

Literacy Coalition, 31

Literacy development, support of children's, 51

Literacy Dictionary, The (Harris & Hodges), 30

Literacy education, needs for, 104

Literacy learning, emphasis of on biliteracy and biculturalism, 22

Literacy logs, 30, 36–37, 79

Literate, differently, 15, 103

Literate persons, definitions of, 101–102

Location of ILP, 32–33

Logan, B., 107

Low test performance, 54

Lubeck, S., 15

Lynch, E. W., 85

M

McCarthey, S. J., 87

McDonald, B., 1, 2

McHugh, J., 83

McKay, L. J., 26

McMahon, S. I., 51

Maritza (case study), 67–70

Marliave, R., 33

Marshall, S., 25

Maruyama, G., 25

Mason, J. M., 28

Mazzeo, J., 1

Mehan, H., 15, 18

Melzi, G., 59, 108

Mental modeling, 27

Metacognitive abilities, development of, 26

Mexican American families, 11–12

Michalove, B., 88, 112

Minority group socialization practices, 13

Minority students, 1, 14

Model goals of National Center for Family Literacy, 16

Moll, L. C., 14, 18, 22, 23, 25, 29, 87, 102, 103, 107

Monitoring learning, 51–52

Moore, J. E., 33

Moran, C. E., 24

Morrow, L. M., 28, 100

Mulhern, M., 17, 18

Multiliteracies, definition, 5

Multiple literacies, 44–46, 106

Muñoz, C., 1

Murphy, S., 100

N

National Assessment of Educational Progress (NAEP), 1

National Center for Children in Poverty, 2

National Center for Education Statistics, 1, 110

National Center for Family Literacy, 16, 107

National School Lunch Program, 2

Neff, D., 14, 29, 87, 103

Nelson, D., 25

New London Group, 5

Newmann, F. M., 30, 55

Non-middle class homes, literacy practices in, 87–88

O

Oakes, J., 1, 25

Office of Governmental and Interagency Affairs, 83

Oral and written discourse experiences, 29

Orfield, G., 26

Origins of ILP, 18

Outcomes
of case studies, 58–59
data on Parents as Classroom Storybook Readers Project, 90
factors explaining positive ILP, 107
Home Literacy Portfolio Project, 92, 95

programmatic and learning, 58–67
summary of ILP, 81–82

P

Palmer, D. J., 27

Paratore, J. R., 26, 58, 59, 89, 91, 95, 100, 108

Pardo, L., 51

Parent-child interaction in Mexican American families, 11–12

Parent-child literacy interaction, 64, 65

Parent-child read-alouds, 91

Parent involvement
advocacy of, 4
definition, 84
importance of, 83
projects for support of, 99
studies on program support of, 86

Parents
absence of resources for children of undereducated, 16
attitudes toward education of, 109–110
audiotapes of parent-child read-alouds, 91
boundaries between school/parent roles, 12
changes in literacy of, 63–64, 63–67
effective engagement of, 112
empowering, ways of, 17
failure to attend/participate in school activities by, 98–99
Hispanic, 110
importance of introducing to reading/writing practices, 29
impression of about children's academic performance, 65
with limited formal schooling, insights gained into, 92
meeting needs of, 104–105
Mexican, 11
perception of school versus family roles, 12
perception of their roles/responsibilities, 84–85
reports of children's school achievement by, 67

reports of intimidation felt by, 89
roles of, 27–28, 84–85, 109
separated view of home and
school by, 84–85
for strategies, 94
task of, 93–94
teachers' beliefs about versus
reality, 110
teachers' interpretations of
behavior of, 112
ways of using literacy by, 111
Parents as Classroom Storybook
Readers Project, 89–92, 99,
110
Parents' literacy, changes in, 63–64
Parents' reports, of children's
school achievement, 67
Paris, S. G., 26–27, 33, 39
Parra, E., 85
Pearson, P. D., 39
Pease-Alvarez, L., 13–14, 15, 107,
110
Pellegrini, A. D., 28, 46
Personal narratives, 40–41, 42–44.
See also Journal entries
Portfolio approach to assessment,
30, 44, 56
Predictive value of factors for
children's success, 111
Preparation for early reading
instruction, 28
Pressley, M., 27
Printed label for child's school
record, 51
Program completion, 56
Programmatic outcomes, 58–67
Programs. *See also* Intergenerational Literacy Project
(ILP)
disagreements about
goals/purposes of, 100
early intervention, 15–16
evaluation, ILP's, 53–54
Even Start, 107
family-based intervention, 13,
54–55
family literacy, 2, 16–17, 17–18,
103, 104–108
instruction for parents in sharing
storybooks, 23
parent involvement support,
studies on, 86

reciprocity in intergenerational
learning, 2
research studies on effects of, 86
two-generation, 2
Project FLAME, 17–18
Projects, influence of on teachers'
perceptions, 110–111
Purcell-Gates, V., 7, 15, 28–29, 54,
103
Purpose of ILP, 88–89
Purves, A. C., 6

Q

Questions raised for goals of family
literacy intervention, 109
Quigley, Andrew, 19
Quintero, E., 18

R

Radencich, M. C., 26
Raphael, T. E., 51
Read-aloud sessions, 91, 92
Readers, experiences of early versus
nonearly, 28
Reading, preparation for, 38–39
Reading achievement, 2
Reading lessons, 35, 38–39
Reading proficiency, grouping
students by, 25–26
Reading strategies, definition, 26
Reciprocity, 2, 14–15, 87
Recognition perspective, 14
Recognition stage of metacognitive
development, 27
Recruiting families for ILP, 32
Regulation stage of metacognitive
development, 27
Research studies. *See also* Case
studies; Statistics
African American children in
urban poverty, 8–9
basic findings across a series of,
14–15
bilingualism and literacy skills
(Mexican American families),
11–12
effects of programs for
supporting parent
involvement, 86
high/low-income families, 15
home literacy of children in low-
income families, 28–29

improving comprehension, 27
influence of bilingualism on
cognition, 24
Latino families (town of
Portillo), 9–10
middle/low-socioeconomic
families, 84–85
nonmainstream families, 85
outcomes of Project Flame, 18
working class communities
(towns of Roadville/
Trackton), 8
young fluent readers, 28
Resources, absence of for children
of undereducated parents, 16
Responding to reading selections,
39–40
Responsibilities, parents'
perceptions of, 84–85
Retention rates, 62, 82n1
Roadville (town of, case study), 8
Rodríquez-Brown, F. V., 17, 18
Role plays, 94
Roles
boundaries between school/
parent, 12
family, of ILP participants, 57
of homework in home literacy,
10
of parents in children's reading,
27–28
of parents in learning, 109
parents' perceptions of, 84–85

S

Sable, J., 110
St. Pierre, R. G., 1, 62
Samples. *See* Examples
Sandler, H. M., 84
Santiago-Santiago, I., 1
Scarborough, H. S., 28
Schieffelin, B., 24
School literacy, learning about,
108–109
School reform model, 86–87
Schools, messages to parents via
actions of, 11
Scott, J., 28, 46
Scribner, S., 103
Sears, D., 21
Secada, W. G., 1
Segal, M., 85

Self-monitoring, 44–51
Serpell, R., 55, 111
Shanahan, T., 17, 18
Shannon, P., 15, 100, 104, 107, 110
Shannon, S. M., 13–14
Sharan, S., 25
Shockley, B., 88, 112
Silber, J., 19, 21–22
Silvia (case study), 76–80
Slavin, R., 1, 25
Small-group discussions, 107
Small groups for reading the
    selection, 39
Social change perspective, 104–105
Socialization, minority group, 13
Social relationships, 26
Social responsibility, 6
Sociocultural learning, principles
    of, 23–24
Staffing, ILP's, 107
Stages of metacognitive
    development, 27
Statistics. *See also* Research studies
    City of Chelsea demographics,
        20–21
    English usage, 25
    enrollment, 1
    families participating in ILP,
        57–58
    outcomes of ILP participation,
        81–82
    race/gender, 4
    school success/failure, reasons
        for, 109
Stein, R. C., 85
Stennett, J., 110
Sticht, T. G., 1, 2, 62
Storybook reading, 46
Strategies. *See also* Parents as
    Classroom Storybook Readers
    Project
    bilingual/bicultural/biliterate
        approaches, 107
    cognitively oriented, to
        reading/writing, 22
    definition of reading, 26
    formal/informal, 102–103
    learned and practiced in
        storybook reading sessions, 91
    for parents, 94
    reading, 26, 38

Street, B., 101
Strickland, D., 54
Students, grouping by reading
    proficiency, 25–26
Students, minority, 1, 14
Studies. *See* Case studies; Research
    studies
Successful learners, characteristics
    of versus moderate learners,
    59–60
Summary of case studies, 80–81
Summary of findings of ILP study,
    81–82
Suro, R., 110
Swadener, B. B., 15
Swanson, B. B., 25
Swap, S. M., 88, 100
Swartz, J., 62

T
Tao, F., 62
Tarr, H., 62
Taylor, D., 2, 7, 8, 9, 15, 24, 29, 54,
    110
Teacher-child ratio in child care
    center, 50
Teachers
    acknowledgment by, of children's
        literacies, 29
    assumptions of, 99
    beliefs of about parents versus
        reality, 110
    building upon biliterate-
        bicultural backgrounds of,
        34
    children's school achievement
        reports, 66
    effective engagement of, 112
    importance of actions of, 85–88
    interpretations of parents'
        behavior by, 112
    projects, influence of on
        perceptions of, 110–111
    tasks of, 94–95
Texts, commonly used, 35
Tharp, R. G., 26, 39, 107
Theoretical assumptions of ILP,
    54–56
Think-alouds, 27
Thornburg, D. G., 18
Tierney, R. J., 30

Topics of journal entries, frequent,
    42
Tracey, D., 100
Trackton (town of, case study), 8
Transcript of conversation about
    family literacy portfolios,
    95–98
Turner, J. C., 26–27
Two-generation programs, 2

U
Undereducation, intergener-
    ational, 3

V
Valdés, G., 4, 6, 9, 11–13, 15, 29,
    95, 110
Van Ijzendoorn, M. H., 28, 46
Vasquez, O., 13–14, 15, 107,
    110
Velarde, M. C., 18
Vélez-Ibáñez, C. G., 87
Venezky, R. L., 33
Villanueva, L., 15
Voelkl, K. E., 1
Vygotsky, L. S., 23, 39

W
Wagner, D., 4, 5, 6
Wasik, B. A., 26–27
Weber, R. M., 24
Welfare dependency, 3
Wellman, H. M., 27
Whitehurst, G. J., 29
Wilkinson, I., 28, 46
Winfield, L., 33
Wixson, K. K., 39
Wolf, D. P., 30
Words, importance of, 100–103
Workforce Investment Act of 1988,
    100–101
Writing evaluation rubric (sample),
    128
Writing journals. *See* Journal
    entries
Writing lessons, 41–44
Written and oral discourse
    experiences, 29

Y
Yun, J. T., 26